She Came From Hell

Jessica Stoner

Published by Trellis Publishing, 2021.

SHE CAME FROM HELL

First edition. July 14, 2021.

ISBN: 979-8224638604

Written by Jessica Stoner.

SHE CAME FROM HELL

JESSICA STONER

When James "Reggie" and Carol Sumner moved to Jacksonville, Florida for their retirement, they had visions of good health and happiness. They never thought that their overnight invitation to long-time South Carolina neighbor, Tiffany Cole, would end up the way it did; With the Sumner couple being buried alive.

Reggie and Carol Sumner were high school sweethearts in North Charleston, South Carolina. They were the kind of couple that everyone envied as they walked down the hall. Unfortunately, their lives pulled them in different directions. Reggie decided to serve his country in the navy. After finishing his tour, he got married and landed a job with the railroad. Carol also married and became a devoted mother, however, her first marriage ended in divorce, and her second nearly killed her. In 1987, after years of abuse, her husband at the time shot her seven times in their home before driving away and turning the gun on himself. Her daughter, Rhonda Alford, just ten years old at that time, spent almost a year helping her mother recover from her wounds. She had to help her bathe, dress, and take care of the house. After taking eight years to fully recover, Carol went back to work as soon as she was able. For over twenty-five years she was a civil servant at the Citadel and the Charleston Air Force Base. She also worked a second job at night at a Belk department store, among other jobs she would take when needed. She did whatever she had to in order to make ends meet. Shortly after her recovery, she found out that the blood transfusion she had received during her previous trauma had given her Hepatitis C. She was angry because she felt as though she could not escape her late ex-husband, but she refused to let it ruin her life. She soon started a new job at a cable company and it was during this time that her life finally changed for the better. Nearly forty years after they'd left high school, a chance encounter brought Carol and Reggie together again. One night in 2000, a phone call was made to the cable company where Carol was working, which she received. After talking with the customer Carol and learning his name, she realized that he also sounded just like the Reggie she remembered. So she asked him if he was the same Reggie Sumner who attended Garrett High school in South Charleston. It was. They decided that they should get together after not seeing each other in so long. This time, though they were inseparable. Like "teenagers in love", a quick courtship led to love and then marriage in 2001 with a ceremony at Carol's home in West Ashley. Carol's daughter has said of Reggie "he was just a very gentle, kind and giving spirit. You could not ask for a better friend, husband or stepfather." Eventually, after retiring, the couple decided to move from South Carolina to Jacksonville, Florida. Reggie had previously bought a house during his days working for CSX railroad and as he was a "brittle" diabetic in frail health, he thought he would be more comfortable in the warmer climate. Carol agreed. "She only went down there to honor her husband," Rhonda said. Before moving, they decided to sell their Chevrolet Lumina to the stepdaughter of a friend who lived down the street, Tiffany Cole. They allowed her to make payments on the car to help her out and she agreed, often driving down to Jacksonville with friends to make those payments. Tiffany and the Sumners became friends and Tiffany would often spend the night at their house when she and her friends went down south. A pleasant girl on the outside, the Sumners had no idea what Tiffany could really be like.

Tiffany Ann Cole was born on December 3, 1981, to her sixteen-year-old mother, Shirley Duncan. Her biological father was in jail. She had no male role model to look up to or who could offer her protection the way a father should. Her mother had a boyfriend, but he was beyond cruel and especially loved to torment Tiffany. At one point, she had a puppy which her stepdad threw against a wall, breaking its neck right in front of her. He was abusive verbally as well as physically and Tiffany claims that as a young girl, he began to molest her, beginning around age eight. As a young teenager, she turned to alcohol and drugs to deal with the pain. In high school, Tiffany was a student who participated in cheerleading and played the flute. She was also a girl scout member but eventually the alcohol and drugs took over her life and she quit her programs and dropped out of school. At one point she fell in love with a boy with severe epilepsy, who ended up breaking her heart and since the only example of love from a man came from an abusive stepfather, this breakup reinforced the belief that she should expect to be treated badly and let down by men. She began looking for love in all the wrong places. In May of 2005, during a six-month period of prostitution, Tiffany ran into a man by the name of Michael Jackson. They were drawn to each other right away and began to get high and sleep together.

Michael James Jackson, born May 12, 1982, had a significant criminal history beginning in childhood. Born to a drug-addicted mother, he was mostly raised by his grandmother. He had multiple felony convictions but only for things like fraud and theft. After meeting Tiffany and becoming close, they took a road trip, first going to Myrtle Beach, then driving to Jacksonville, Florida, where they would be staying with Michael's best friend, Alan Wade. Born May 22, 1987, Alan and Michael had known each other for just over a year. When Tiffany and Michael arrived in Florida, they stayed at Alan's mom's house. After just a few days, though, she kicked them out because she was tired of the loud noises and constant partying. With nowhere else to go and with all their money spent on the nights of drinking and partying, Tiffany remembered that the Sumners lived nearby. The three friends showed up at their doorstep and explained what had happened. The couple was very happy to see Tiffany and invited her and her friends to stay the night. While they were chatting and catching up, Carol mentioned how worried they had been about their house in North Carolina not selling. There was no need to worry, however, because not only did their property sell, but they had also made a $99,000 profit. It was this general statement to a long-time neighbor that sealed the Sumner's fate.

It's difficult to know just whose idea it was to rob the Sumner's. Some say it was both Tiffany and Michael, while others say it was Michael who was the plan maker and master manipulator. Either way, a plan was hatched to rob and kill the loving couple. At some point in June, Alan had contacted his friend, Bruce Nixon Jr., and told him of a plan to rob someone. No other details were given. Then on July 6th, Alan called Bruce, born May 9th, 1987, and asked him if he would be interested in joining the others in digging a hole. Bruce agreed and stole four shovels from his neighborhood. The other three friends drove to Bruce's house in a rented Mazda RX-8 that Tiffany had rented in South Carolina. The group drove around hoping to find a perfectly remote place for the hole to be dug. Alan asked Bruce if he knew of any good places to which Bruce responded that he did. He took them into Georgia, to a wooded area just over the state line. Leaving the car parked on the road, the group walked through the wooded area into a clearing where they began to dig a hole while Tiffany held a flashlight. It was approximately four feet deep and six feet square. Upon completion of the hole, they left the shovels and went back to the car. It was here that Alan asked Michael if Bruce could join in on their robbery plan. Michael agreed. The foursome drove back to Alan's house but his mother would not allow Michael in as she believed him to be a bad influence on her son. Over the next couple of days, it was Tiffany's job to remain in contact with Carol and Reggie in order to gain information from them about their plans and whereabouts. The foursome also secretly watched the house in order to figure out the Sumner's routine. It was unclear yet as to whether or not the group would enter the home while the couple was gone or if they would simply go in with the couple there. It was ultimately decided that they would enter the home while the couple was there so that they could get their financial information and the means to access their accounts. Michael said that he would kill the victims by injecting them with a lethal dose of their medications. He then promised that the four friends would split the money they received from the Sumner's accounts, each receiving about $50,000. They began making preparations for their plan. Just after midnight on July 8th, 2005, Michael, Tiffany, and Alan went to Wal-Mart and purchased disposable rubber gloves. On the evening of the murders, they went to an Office Depot, where Tiffany bought duct tape and a large roll of plastic wrap. Last, they bought a toy gun that shot plastic pellets.

Around 10pm., on July 8th, 2005, Tiffany drove the other three group members to the Sumner's house in the Mazda. Herself and Michael remained in the car while Alan and Bruce went up to the door. They had the duct tape and toy gun and both were wearing the plastic gloves. After Carol answered the door, Bruce and Alan told her that they were having car trouble and asked if they could use their phone. Carol said of course they could and invited them in. As soon as the boys entered the home, Alan pulled the phone cord out of the wall. Bruce pointed the gun at the couple. Alan grabbed Reggie around the neck and pushed him down into a chair. They told the couple that they wanted credit and debit cards and any other financial information. Carol began pleading with the boys not to hurt them. Bruce took the couple into a spare bedroom where he used duct tape to bind their legs and hands and to cover their mouths and eyes. Alan sent a text message to Michael, informing him that everything was under control. Michael then also entered the home and he and Alan began searching for financial information. They saw a pile of mail and financial statements which they put into a plastic bag. They spotted Reggie's prized coin collection and took that too. Michael told the other two to take the couple into the garage at which point they put them into the trunk of the Lincoln Town car. Tiffany went into the house and grabbed some of their belongings, put them into a bag and took the bag with her to the Mazda. Following the plan, both cars headed towards the gravesite, stopping only once to put gas in the Lincoln. Upon arrival at the site, Michael opened the trunk and apparently began screaming when he saw that the duct tape had become loose and the couple had worked the tape off. It had been over 100 degrees in the trunk. Sweat had caused the tape to loosen. They had also taken the tape off their eyes and were huddled together. Michael ordered Bruce to tape them up again, which he did. Alan then attempted to back up the car to the edge of the grave but, unable to do so, Bruce took over. Michael then sent Bruce up the road to wait with Tiffany at the Mazda. While still alive, the Sumners were taken out of the trunk and pushed into the hole. It is unclear as to who actually did the burying because Alan and Michael each blamed the other. Somehow, Michael ended up getting the personal identification number of the Sumner's bank account. Reports differ on whether he obtained this information from somewhere in the house or if Carol told him the number while being threatened to be buried alive. According to one documentary, Carol had gotten the tape off her mouth again when in the hole. Michael was telling them that if they didn't give up their PIN, they would die, at which point Carol yelled it out. It didn't seem to matter either way though because they continued to shovel dirt onto the scared couple.

After filling the hole, Alan and Michael put the shovels back into the trunk of the Lincoln and drove it up the road to where Tiffany and Bruce were waiting with the Mazda. The four of them drove to Sanderson, Florida, where they abandoned the Lincoln after wiping it clean of fingerprints. They then drove back to Jacksonville where they immediately went to an ATM and withdrew money from the Sumner's account, before retiring to a hotel. Alan and Tiffany went to another Wal-Mart where they purchased more latex gloves as well as bleach. They returned to the Sumner's home in order to clean up any evidence. They also stole a computer. Bruce stayed with the group for another day and then went home, but Alan remained with Michael and Tiffany who returned to South Carolina, where Tiffany rented two hotel rooms; one for herself and Michael and one for Alan. It should be noted that after returning home, Bruce went to a party with a plastic bag filled with different medications. At one point he announced that he had found a new job murdering people. He stated that he had buried people alive and killed them without mentioning the involvement of anyone else.

On the morning of July 10th, Carol's daughter, Rhonda, decided to report to police the fact that she hadn't been able to get hold of her mother for a few days. Since they kept in touch on a regular basis and spoke every couple days, it was highly unusual for her mother to not return her calls. The next day, the Jacksonville Sheriff's Office (JSO) went to the Sumner's home. The back door of the house was unlocked and in the kitchen there dirty after-dinner plates, which was also highly unusual for the couple. The JSO began to investigate the financial accounts of the couple and they found that large amounts of money had been withdrawn within a short time frame. Video footage from the ATM machines that the group had used showed Michael's face and the silver Mazda in the background. On July 12th, after Rhonda made a plea on local TV networks for the safe return of her parents, the Sheriff's office received a phone call from someone posing as Reggie Sumner. Dispatch contacted Detective David Meacham of the Sheriff's office and put the caller through.

Meacham: Where are you at?

Michael: We're in Delaware right now

Meacham: And what city is that in?

Michael: It's in Corpus

Meacham: Corpus, Delaware?

Michael: Yes

However, the town of Corpus, Delaware does not exist. Next, Tiffany came on the phone posing as Carol.

Meacham: Is this Carol?

Tiffany: Yes, sir, it is.

Meacham: Okay. This is Detective Meacham from the Sheriff's office. How are you doing tonight?

Tiffany: I was sleeping

Meacham: I understand. I understand you have some health problems

Tiffany: Mmhmm

Meacham: Okay. Any other problems?

Tiffany: I'm really tired right now

Meacham: What kind of problems do you have?

Tiffany: Cancer

Meacham: Cancer?

Tiffany: Mmhmm

The detective called Rhonda into the station so that she could listen to the taped conversation. She confirmed that the people posing as the Sumners were definitely not Carol and Reggie. The main reason for the call was to ensure everyone that the Sumners were alive and well and because the bank accounts had been frozen. They asked the detectives to reinstate the accounts, which they did so that they could track the money in order to locate the perpetrators. They also had the phone number from which Michael had called. Using this information, they were able to find that the phone was registered to Michael and that a call had been placed to a car rental agency in Charleston. They also learned that the cell had been used near the Sumner's home the night of the murders. Detective Meacham contacted the rental company and was told that the car had been rented to a Tiffany Cole and that it was overdue. Using the rental car's GPS system, they were able to find that the car had also been near the Sumner's residence during the time of the abduction. Using the cell phone trace, the car's GPS and the photos of Michael at different ATMs, police were able to locate the general whereabouts of the three murderers. On July 14th, with help from Tiffany's brother, who was on probation and threatened with jail, police raided a Best Western hotel in Charleston and arrested Tiffany

Cole, Alan Wade, and Michael Jackson. Bruce Nixon was also picked up at his home in Florida.

While Tiffany, Michael, and Alan refused to cooperate with law enforcement, Bruce appeared to have some semblance of a conscience because he broke down and admitted to the crimes right away. He also agreed to lead police to the burial site. For the first time in TV history, documentary footage showed Bruce and detectives at the grave site where Bruce broke down in sobs. Excavation of the site began the next day. The victims were found fully clothed in a crouching position. Reggie had somehow broken his tape and was holding Carol's hand. There was two feet of dirt over their heads. With ten years of homicide under his belt, Detective Meacham said it was one of the saddest and most horrible things he had ever seen. The medical examiner determined that both Reggie and Carol were alive in the hole before they were buried. Their nostrils, mouths, throats, esophagi, and trachea had fine sprays of dirt in them, which indicated that they had inhaled it. They died from mechanical asphyxiation and smothering, caused by the dirt covering their heads while compressing their chests. She said it was the worst case of asphyxiation she'd ever seen. It was "horrendous."

At some point while in jail, but unaware that Bruce had come clean, Michael's grandmother called him.

Grandma: Michael, listen to me and don't say a word. You're in the newspaper. All over the newspaper yesterday and today

Michael: For what?

Grandma: Murder

Michael: What?!

Grandma: Murder. 'Bodies ID'd as former South Carolina couple James and Carol Sumner. Bail was denied for 18-year-old Bruce Nixon of Florida who was arrested and charged with murder, home invasion, robbery, and kidnapping.' He took them to the grave site and everything

Michael: Oh my God. Are you kidding me?

Grandma: It's right here in today's paper

Michael: Bruce took them to the f*****g spot. The f****r showed them where the spot was at?

Grandma: Yes, dear

Michael: *starts panting* Bruce just killed us all

Bruce Nixon told detectives everything that had happened and agreed to testify on behalf of the prosecution. He wasn't sentenced until after he testified against the other three group members, but in the end, he received 45 years for each victim, currently being served concurrently at Century Correctional Institution in Florida. Alan Wade was tried first.

Michael Jackson was the first to be tried. Testifying on his own behalf, Michael stated that the plan was only to rob the Sumners and that it was not going to involve murder. He said that Alan and Bruce went into the house and when they came out they drove off in the Lincoln which he then followed. He claims he had no idea that Reggie and Carol were in the trunk. According to Michael, when they arrived at the hole in Georgia, it was Alan and Bruce who told him where to park and to bring them a flashlight. It was when he arrived at the burial site that he heard Carol moan. He then stated that he questioned what the other two were doing before returning to the Mazda to wait. He did admit to impersonating Reggie. Bruce testified that Michael had been the ringleader and was the one who orchestrated everything. After stepping down from the witness stand, Carol's daughter, Rhonda, said of Bruce, "I just wanted to hug him. He is a murderer, but in the end, he did the right thing." It was that testimony that she believed sealed Michael's fate because he was found guilty of first degree murder, robbery, and kid-napping, and sentenced to death for each murder. He is currently on death row in Florida.

Alan was next to be tried. Two witnesses who were not identified gave victim impact statements during the penalty phase. Alan's lawyer then called six of their own witnesses to testify including Bruce Nixon,

Alan's mom and sister, the mother of a friend, his middle school principal, and his youth pastor. Overall, the witnesses testified that Alan's parents divorced when he was eight and his father disappeared from his life. His mother took him to church regularly and as a kid, he was kind, smart, and well-behaved. After the divorce, his mother was unable to spend a lot of time with him because she had to work a lot to support them. When he was in his teens, his mother had a bout with breast cancer. By his early teens, he began to use drugs. In the sixth grade, he was involuntarily committed to a 72-hour hold because of a drug related incident. When he was sixteen, his mom had to take him out of school or be arrested for his truancy. The next year, his mother kicked him out of the house in an attempt at tough love because his drug use was becoming worse. In 2004 Alan introduced her to Michael, whom she immediately saw as a bad influence on him. Since his arrest and before his trial, Alan had apparently become a model prisoner, obtained his G.E.D and tutored other inmates in math. Nothing seemed to sway the jury, however, because he was found guilty on all counts and voted eleven-to-one to receive the death penalty. He is also currently on death row in Florida.

Tiffany was the last to be tried. Her lawyer argued that she wasn't a major participant in the crimes. He said that she was under the control of her boyfriend Michael, and that he was the mastermind. Tiffany claimed that she believed the crime would only constitute a simple theft and that she didn't knowingly participate in the robberies, kidnapping or murders. She insisted that she did not know that Reggie and Carol were in the trunk of the Lincoln until they arrived at the burial site. The circuit judge, Michael Weatherby did not see it that way, stating that it was she who held the flashlight during the digging of the grave and was there when they were bound and placed in the trunk. He also noted that she was the one who purchased the duct tape and gloves and later pawned the jewelry and computer they had stolen. "She was thoroughly involved," Weatherby stated. "She knew exactly what she was doing and participated without hesitation." It was noted as well that she was the only one of the four who had previously known the Sumners. During the penalty phase, the prosecution called two of the victim's family members who gave impact statements. The defense attorney then called up witnesses who testified that Tiffany was of good character. Three of those witnesses were correctional officers who stated that Tiffany had been no trouble in jail and did not cause any problems. A psychiatrist, Dr. Earnest Miller, testified that she suffered from poly-substance and alcohol abuse, chronic depression, and a personality disorder. He also stated that she had witnessed abuse to family members and had been sexually abused herself by her stepfather. On the other hand, he testified that Tiffany was competent and thus he could not support a plea of insanity. Finally, he stated that she knew right from wrong and had a high average IQ. In the end, Tiffany was also found guilty of all charges and sentenced to death by a 9-3 vote. Upon hearing her fate, she bowed her head and turned to her mother, mouthing the words "I love you". Her lawyer, Quentin Till, said she had been ready for the decision. He visited her in jail that week. "I told her to be strong," he said. "...I still see her being utilized and manipulated by Michael Jackson." Revis Sumner, Reggie's brother, said that Tiffany has since written to the family, asking for forgiveness. He says he has forgiven her, but that doesn't mean she shouldn't suffer for her actions. The Reverend Jean Clark, Reggie's sister has said, "I pray for Tiffany. I pray for all of them. I'm grieved that these four young people have wasted their lives." Chief Assistant State Attorney, Jay Plotkin, who tried all four cases said, "All of these defendants got exactly what they deserved. Justice was done." After the sentences were given and the trials were over, Reggie's son, Frederick Hallock, said, "You expect some sort of closure or some sort of good feeling when the verdict is read, but it didn't seem to help much. I just know they didn't deserve this." Currently, Tiffany is one of only five women on Florida's death row. At the time of her sentence, she was the sole woman there.

Tiffany, Michael, and Alan all filed appeals after their trials, citing multiple issues. All three were denied and their sentences were upheld. Recently, in 2015, Tiffany filed another appeal, asking for a new trial. She claims that her defense lawyers were ineffective and that she should not have been convicted of first-degree murder since she did not actually bury the bodies herself. But according to Florida law, it doesn't matter who actually committed the murder. Just knowing that it was going to happen is enough to warrant a guilty verdict. At her original trial Tiffany said, "But please remember I didn't do this. I am not the monster that created this, but I regret meeting him," referring to Michael. Upon hearing that Tiffany was asking for a new trial, Reggie's sister, Jean had this to say: "Most people are going to try to come back with something like that after the fact, because they're going to try to find a loophole and get off. But justice has a voice, and justice has to be served." And the thought of going through another trial breaks her heart. "I have family members that are still not the same and never will be the same. In fact, I don't like to involve them too much into things like this, because they can't deal with it."

In 2014, Alan Wade also filed an appeal for a new trial, citing that his lawyers did not do a good job of representing him. His appellate lawyers said that his original defense lawyers barely met with him before the trial and didn't interview witnesses prior to putting them on the stand. They also cited the lack of objections to supposedly questionable evidence. In December 2014, it was decided by the Supreme Court of Florida that his conviction be upheld.

Previous to that, Michael Jackson filed an appeal for a new trial, stating that his lawyers were also ineffective. As with Alan's trial, Michael claims that his lawyers did not make objections to certain evidence when there was clearly an objection to be made. The judge did allow an appeal hearing for his concerns and at the close of the hearing, Michael was allowed to make a statement. It went as follows:

First, I'd like to say that I am guilty of the crimes of first-degree murder, kidnapping, and robbery against Mr. and Mrs. Sumner. My reason for wanting to address the Court today is because of the many lies I told to everyone years ago at pretrial and then trial. I downplayed my involvement to look as if I were not guilty but the truth is that—the truth is that it was my idea to do this. Truly, I did not make anyone do anything. All were willing participants but I was, in fact, the leader. It was my idea to do it. I lied to this Court all throughout my trial testimony, same to [defense counsel and the State]. Even more so I lied to the people who deserve the truth the most, the family of Mr. and Mrs. Sumner, and for that, I am deeply sorry. There are no words that I could ever offer that would convey the depth of my remorse or sorrow, but again I say that I am truly sorry for what I have done and though I'm undeserving, I do ask forgiveness. My desire today is to reconcile the truth to the family of Mr. and Mrs. Sumner and to Your Honor, the attorneys and to the Court record. If necessary, I will answer any and all questions fully and truthfully. Thank you.

His conviction was upheld. Tiffany, Michael, Alan, and Bruce remain in jail today, with the former three on death row.

"It's sad," said Rhonda Alford about her parents. "It took them so long to find each other." Carol and Reggie's ashes sit in an urn in Rhonda's home, forever mixed and blended together.

KILLER TWINS : THE TRUE STORY OF THE WHITEHEADS

17

AMY AILIS

Tasmiyah and Jasmiyah Whitehead

" I know what Nikki wanted for them and that's why it's so shocking that they're in prison when they should be in college living their lives. And just knowing that the last thing she saw was her children murdering her, it hurts me to my soul just to know that she had to go through that. She didn't deserve that – nobody does." Sylvia Renee Shields – Nikki's friend.[1]

Jarmecca Yvonne Whitehead, known as Nikki to her friends and family, was born on April 18th, 1975 to her mother, Lynda. It wasn't the best start in life – Nikki was born in prison while Lynda was incarcerated for robbery, and a drug offence, in the mid-1970s.[2]

Nikki was raised by her grandmother, Della Frazier. Della hadn't had the easiest of upbringings herself – her own mother had suffered a nervous breakdown when Della was 12. So when Lynda gave birth to Nikki in prison, Della took her in and raised her, having already raised two daughters and a son of her own.[3]

Nikki fell pregnant when she was 17 and the father, a Jamaican national, was not in the picture for long.

Nikki's best friend, Sylvia Shields, recalled *"She was huge, her stomach was really really huge...It was so funny because we were all like 'God this is going to be a big baby.'"*

In 1993 Nikki delivered a baby girl after several hours of labor.

"After the first baby came...you're expecting the placenta to come next...it was another baby. Everybody was in shock, basically, because nobody knew she was having twins."

Nikki's brother, Haneef, was also surprised by the double arrival.

"One was hiding behind the other one...and you could only see one heartbeat. It was like...whoa...everybody was happy."

Nikki named her new baby girls Tasmiyah and Jasmiyah, or Tas and Jas, and felt that they were a new start, a chance to start over after her sometimes troubled upbringing.

It wasn't going to be easy for the teenager, not only was she now a single mom, but she was a single mom to two babies. She knew there would be challenges but she was determined to be the best mother she could.

The three of them – Nikki, Tas and Jas, lived at Della's house with the ageing grandmother.

The Twins

Right from the start, the two little girls were inseparable.

"Ever since those girls were born they were extremely close...you couldn't separate one without the other. It's like they fed off of each other almost" recalled Sylvia Shields.

Haneef continued *"They always whispered in each other's ears...I thought that's what girls do...what twins do. They finished each other's sentences..."*

Fred Rosen, the author of *Trails of Death*, observed that it was a very dependent relationship. *"There was something very primal about the way these kids grew up and got into each other."*

As the girls grew up, Nikki noticed that her daughters were extremely clever girls, and very talented. Nikki wanted to nurture that talent, so she gave the girls everything they wanted. They were enrolled in singing lessons, dancing lessons, and both girls learnt to play musical instruments.[4]

A Different Story

However, Nikki's grandmother, Della Frazier, told a different story to the one of the doting mother.

She recalled that, when Nikki fell pregnant, she was living away from home and was not at all prepared for motherhood. When the twins were born, though, Nikki went back home to Della's and the three of them moved in.

She paints a slightly different picture of Nikki.

"Nikki was a person who liked to go, and she stayed gone all the time ... and she got in the wrong lifestyle, she started doing drugs and drinking and got in with the wrong people."

Della also denied that it was Nikki who gave the girls the extra-curricular lessons they so enjoyed. According to her, it was she and her husband, who died in 2009, who paid for the twins' upbringing with little input from Nikki.

"I was still raising her — and her children."

Della was working full-time at the Coca-Cola Company, but despite this, she said she enjoyed the company of the twins and that they were well-behaved, polite, and courteous towards her.[5]

Robert Head

One day in 2000, while Nikki was out shopping at the mall, she was spotted by a man named Robert Head.

"I was sitting on the fountain, one afternoon, about 6 o clock...Nikki came into the mall. I said 'I just can't let her get away.'"

55-year-old Robert, although 30 years older than Nikki, would not be put off and he persuaded Nikki to go out on a date with him that same night. The couple went to dinner and then he took her dancing.

Robert spoiled Nikki, whom he described as his movie star. He treated her like a lady and bought her nice things.

He lived in a gated community in Conyers, roughly 25 miles from Atlanta, and it wasn't long before Nikki moved in with him.

Nikki wanted to better herself – she hadn't had the smoothest of starts to life, so, while keeping her job at Decatur's Simply Unique salon, she enrolled at Bauder College, where she studied fashion design.

Ronda Anderson was one of Nikki's tutors, and she said that Nikki stood out, with her sense of passion for whatever she happened to be engaged in.

"That's when I actually learned that Nikki was a hair stylist. I came in the class early one day, as I normally do, and she looked up at me and she said 'Miss Anderson, what's going on with your hair?' And I said 'What? Excuse me?' and then she asked me this question, 'Do you have a hair stylist? And does she know you have your hair looking like that today?' and I said 'Yes. And No.' and she said 'Miss Anderson, I'm giving her one more chance, one more chance, and if it's not right, I'm taking over.'"

The Twins at School

Whether it was Nikki, or her grandmother, Della, who put the girls in dance and singing classes, the girls excelled.

Katie Beck, a reporter with NBC Affiliate WXIA who worked on the story, said that the girls were well loved by their teachers.

"Their teachers described them as almost angelic...sweet...happy and engaged and there's pictures of them...one on each of Nikki's arms. Teachers described them that way... that they had a sweet demeanour in their classrooms and with their classmates, and they were almost timid."[6]

But something was about to change.

One Big Happy Family

By 2007 Nikki's life was sorted. She had her career, a good boyfriend, and a home in a safe area – exactly the kind of stability she wanted for her girls. So she decided that Jas and Tas should come and live with her and Robert in Conyers.

According to Della, it was Nikki's mother, Lynda, who put pressure on Nikki to bring the girls home, probably due to her own guilt at not having raised Nikki herself.

And also, according to Della, that is when the twins began to change.

The girls were 13 when they moved from their Great Grandmother's house to Robert's home in Conyers. Up until that time, according to their teachers and indeed their own Great Grandmother, the girls were 'perfect'.

But as they entered their teens their behaviour began to change.[7]

"Tas has a more dominating personality, I guess 'cause she's the oldest and Jas always the quiet one." recalls the girls' uncle Haneef.

"While Tas is more aggressive than Jas, at the same time there's something about when they come together, their personalities coalesce...There's a charisma to them but once again that charisma is a joint charisma...it's like putting two isotopes together and you get and atomic bomb" explained Fred Rosen.

As the girls developed, so did their looks and they became beautiful young ladies, but when they started High School the changes became apparent.

"They suddenly are no longer interested in school. These A students who were bound for Harvard are suddenly cutting class." Rosen went on.

So what was it that had turned the heads of the formerly gifted, attentive twins?

In a word - Boys.

Tas and Jas had discovered the opposite sex, but they weren't interested in boys their own age – they were much more interested in boys who were older than them.

Nikki was worried. She was all too aware of what that interest could bring and she wanted to stop her girls making the same mistakes as she had. As a mother, Nikki wanted her daughters to have an education, and see some life, but she knew too well what can happen when a young girl has her head turned by a boy. She was desperate to stop one or both of her daughters falling pregnant at a young age.

But Nikki struggled to control the twins. They began dressing in a way which she felt was too provocative and she started trying to out her foot down.

The girls reacted badly to Nikki's interference, or as they put it, being *"in their business"*.

Psychologist Dr. Becky Beaton explained. *"With Jas and Tas, they're really this raging powder keg of hormones and emotions, and it really plays into their rebelliousness."*

Fred Rosen further explained. *"They're intelligent, and that intelligence enables them to flout the rules and the girls ganged up against their mother."*

On more than one occasion Nikki told the girls they couldn't go out – a fact which didn't go down too well with Jas and Tas. The pair joined forces and pushed back, with Jas telling her Mom *"I can do you...and I can do you better."*

Were those the empty threats of an angry teenager, or would it become a self-fulfilling prophecy?

Things Escalate

In January 2008, Nikki discovered that Tas has been playing truant from school. She was furious – all of her attempts at keeping her daughters under control were being thwarted. She also knew exactly where she would find her wayward daughter – at her boyfriend's house.

Enough was enough as far as Nikki was concerned, and she drove to confront her.

Tas was with her boyfriend when Nikki burst in. She was horrified that her mother had embarrassed her that way, but Nikki didn't care, and dragged her daughter outside and bundled her into the car, confiscating Tas' phone before getting in herself.

The drive home was tumultuous. Tas screamed at her mother for doing what she did, and Nikki resolutely shouted back at Tas, refusing to hand over the cell phone and telling Tas that she could no longer see the 19-year-old boyfriend. With her daughter safely in the car, Nikki had a captive audience – or so she thought.

In the midst of the argument, Tas suddenly opened the passenger side door and jumped out of the moving vehicle. Nikki was horrified – the car had been going at some speed and Tas could have sustained serious injuries.

Nikki stopped the car and ran back to where her daughter lay. Tas was unharmed, but the stunt was a slap in the face to Nikki – it seemed to be Tas' way of telling her mother that she had no hold, no control.

The situation went from bad to worse in the Whitehead home. The two girls developed a routine in which one would be the aggressor towards their mother and the other would pretend to care, flipping roles frequently, playing with their mother's head until she had no idea which, if either, of them she could trust.

The girls were masterful manipulators – so much so that author Fred Rosen remarked that it was the kind of manipulation displayed by criminals.

As the year went on, the twins' behavior became more and more disturbing. Tas started self-harming, and would frequently cut herself.

By that time Nikki was beside herself with worry and fear. And it was that fear for herself and her daughters which led her to seek help in the form of an exorcism.

As Sylvia Shields explained, *"Being black people we are very adamant in our religion and we always be like 'The devil is alive' so she wanted to help them."*

Another of Nikki's friends, Yucca Harris, went on, *"She felt like they were possessed...she enquired about an exorcism for her girls because at some point she felt like it was a darker side to them."*

The exorcism didn't take place – the girls had severe psychological problems but Nikki couldn't, or wouldn't, recognize that fact.

From Bad to Worse

Things didn't improve, and on June 28th, 2008 Nikki found out once again that the girls had been playing truant from school, and yet another argument developed. However, things took a turn for the worse. Jas and Tas both turned on their mother, physically attacking her. Despite it being two against one Nikki managed to break free and ran to her bedroom, where she locked herself in while she called her friend, Sylvia.

"Nikki called me huffing and puffing, crying...I'm saying 'what's wrong with you, what's going on?' and she said she was locked in her room, she said that the girls were trying to fight her. And, she said 'I'm scared' and I said 'if you're scared...call the police.'"

Which is exactly what Nikki did.

The police arrived and heard two very different accounts from Nikki, and the twins.

While Nikki was visibly upset as she described what had been going on, the twins were calm, refuting the allegations and claiming that their mother hated them and that they didn't want to live with her anymore.

The police managed to calm the situation down, and eventually, the trio agreed to call a truce, with the twins promising to go to their rooms and allow things to settle down.

As the family went back inside the house, Police Officer Myra Scruggs decided to stay close.

"I had a bad feeling about them, so I just decided to stay in the neighborhood and was just sitting kind of up from their house."

Inside, Nikki had gone to her bedroom to give herself some breathing space, but as she turned around she was confronted with Tas, who had followed her mother into the bedroom. Tas closed the door, and locked it, before walking towards her mother. As Nikki stood watching her daughter, Tas attacked her again, striking her over and over, while Jas was frantically hammering on the locked door, calling to her mother to let her in so she could help her to get Tas off. Nikki managed to scramble to the door and unlocked it so that Jas could help, but instead of aiding her mother, Jas joined in, and Nikki had both girls beating her up.

Somehow she managed to escape again, and this time she ran to the front door and out into the street. Officer Myra Scruggs heard Nikki screaming, and once again was confronted with Nikki and her daughters. Like earlier on, Nikki described what had happened, while the twins told their version of the story, which was that Nikki had attacked them and not the other way around.

Officer Scruggs examined the girls, and Nikki, and discovered that while Nikki was covered in scratches on her arms, chest, and neck, the girls were unscathed.

"...I had no reason to believe that their mother had attacked them. It was just hard for me to believe that after all my years, that anybody could be that calm, that articulate when they're trying to describe an altercation with their mother, without any emotion. That was just so alarming. They displayed sociopathic behavior...no remorse, no regret...and then I thought it would be best to take them both into custody and I did and off they went."

Juvenile Court

A few days after the twins were taken into custody, they, along with their mother, sat before a juvenile court judge. Nikki told the judge that she couldn't control the girls, and she asked him for help. When it came to the girls' turn, they once again turned the blame on Nikki, labelling her a drug addict who didn't love them anymore.

After listening to both sides, the judge ruled that Nikki was not able to look after her daughters, and sent them to live with Della Frazier, their Great Grandmother. Nikki was hurt that she no longer had custody of her children, but realized that, for the time being, they were better off apart.

This living arrangement was a vast improvement – for the Whitehead twins. Living with their elderly Great Grandmother meant that they had all the freedom in the world, as she was even less able to control them than their mother was.

Haneef Whitehead, Nikki's brother, was horrified. *"When they started staying with my Grandma, she's like, 81 at the time, she can't handle 14-year-old kids, so everything just started boiling over...they were hanging out in the projects 'cause that's where their boyfriends stayed there...they went from her house to staying over at their boyfriend's house and that lasted for like a year and a half..."*

The twins were having the time of their lives. With nobody around to rein them in they ran wild. The one fly in the ointment, though, was the family counselling they had to attend with Nikki every week, as ordered by the court.

The twins used the sessions as an opportunity to let their mother know exactly how they felt – they told her they hated her and never wanted to live with her again, but Nikki loved her daughters and kept insisting she wanted them home.

Return to Court

On December 12th, 2009, after 18 months of living with their Great Grandmother and running wild, the twins were once again back at the family court with Della Frazier, and their mother, Nikki Whitehead.

When asked to explain their continued truancy, the girls denied that they were skipping school, but Della told the judge that she could no longer care for the girls as they were out of control and that something had to be done to bring them back in line.

Nikki stood before the judge and asked him to return the girls to her custody. The twins had told the courts that their mother was using drugs, but a court-ordered drugs test proved negative for every substance. Despite their continued lies and abuse, Nikki did not want her children being turned over to the state and begged the judge to allow them to return home with her.

Nikki won her case and was awarded full custody of her daughters, but as they were leaving the courts Jas told her mother *"If I have to go back with you, I'm going to kill you."*

Homecoming

On Saturday, January 9th, 2010, Nikki threw a homecoming party for the twins. She wanted to make a fresh start, so she had decorated their bedrooms and was excited about them coming back home. Nikki's friends pitched in, knowing how delicate and difficult the situation was.

The girls were not so pleased. On the drive over the girls told Yucca Harris, Nikki's friend, that they didn't want to be going home, and that they didn't want to be at a party with Nikki's other family members.

While Tas joined in, to an extent, at the party, Jas refused to engage at all, and it wasn't long before the girls' old behavior reared its head again, this time in the form of a heated argument with their Aunt, which resulted in the party ending early.

The Aftermath

It was apparent to Nikki that nothing had changed. The twins were still skipping school, going out, and disregarding her rules. Nikki even took to sleeping on the couch in order to stop the girls from leaving the house in the middle of the night. But there was more to it – Nikki also felt safer on the couch than in her own bedroom, where she could be cornered as she had been once before.

Nikki even called Yukka and told her that *"if anything happened to her, the kids did it."*

The Murder

On the morning of January 13th, 2010, Tas and Jas had, once again, gotten up late for school and Nikki was furious. The girls had missed the school bus and a furious row broke out. Neither side was willing to back down and the row escalated to a physical fight, with kitchen utensils, pots, and pans being thrown about.

But then one of the girls picked up a knife and lunged at her mother.

Nikki's arm was slashed and she ran from the house in a panic. There was no answer when she hammered on her neighbor's door. Tas appeared and calmly asked Nikki to come back inside so they could work it out, telling her that everything was going to be ok.

But as Nikki stepped back inside the house, the twins both set on their mother, attacking her and wrestling her to the floor, where they began repeatedly stabbing her, over and over again, in her arm, her neck, her head...wherever the knife landed.

Nikki was stabbed fifty times.

With unrelenting coldness, the twins then dragged their mother into the bathroom and dumped her in the tub before setting about wiping their fingerprints from anything which could tie them to the murder.

They then calmly got dressed, and set off for school, leaving their mother, Nikki, to die alone in the bathroom.

The girls went through the rest of the day as normal. Other students didn't notice anything different about the girls, except for one girl who thought she saw Tas comforting Jas, but it was business as usual for the Whitehead girls.

When the girls got home, they waited by the window until they saw a police car driving past. The girls ran out and flagged the car down, telling the officer inside that they had just come home from school and found their mother dead.

Within minutes the police had descended on the street and cordoned it off as a crime scene.

Lieutenant Chris Moon said, *"You could smell the blood in the air...there was that much blood in the house."*

It was like a scene from a slasher movie.

Inside the house, it was clear that there had been a struggle, and that Nikki had fought for her life. There was blood on the back door, and on the handle, suggesting that Nikki had made it as far as the door before being dragged back in. The couch was soaked in blood, and there was a large pool of blood on the floor, from which drag marks led to the bathroom, where Nikki's body was found floating face-up in the water.

In a small town like Conyers news of the murder spread like wildfire and Sylvia Shields got a call from her mother. *"My mom called me and she said 'you know they found somebody dead in Nikki's neighborhood' I just dropped my head and I said...I said...the twins killed Nikki."*[8]

The girls played the part of the traumatized children well. They told detectives that their mother's bedroom door had been locked when they had left for school at 7.30 that morning and that they had missed the bus and had to walk.

The police knew, or at least suspected, that Nikki's murderer was someone she knew. The rage behind the attack was so savage that Nikki's spinal cord had been severed.

The first person the police wanted to speak to was Nikki's boyfriend, Robert Head, but, at first, they couldn't find him. His absence was explained, however, by his job – he was a long-haul truck driver. Police needed to check his whereabouts on the morning of

Nikki's murder, and eventually, Robert's GPS proved he was a day's drive away when it happened.

With Robert's alibi being watertight, the detectives asked the girls about their mother's friends, people she talked to. Interestingly they discovered that Nikki had a second boyfriend, Joe Carter, who was a barber who worked next door to Nikki's salon. The girls told detectives that they had heard Nikki and Joe arguing on the phone the previous night.

Could a love triangle have been behind Nikki's murder? But, to their surprise, they discovered that there was no secrecy – Robert knew all about Joe, and Nikki had Robert's blessing to date other men when he was away working. He wanted his 'movie star' to be happy, and not lonely when he was on the road.

Joe was questioned as a 'person of interest' – he was examined for signs of a struggle, but there were no such marks on his hands or indeed his body. Furthermore, Joe passed a polygraph test with flying colors – he was not involved in Nikki's murder.

Once again the police turned their attention to other people Nikki knew, including, possibly, a member of Nikki's own family.

It was during these investigations that they learned of the family's troubled past. A 911 call was discovered, in which Nikki, frantic, believed that one of the girls had been abducted in the middle of the night. She hadn't, of course, she had done a moonlight flit to meet a boy.

During one of the interviews with the girls, the detective asked them to remove the gloves they were both wearing. What he saw started alarm bells ringing. Both girls' hands and arms were covered in scratch marks, cuts, and bite marks – injuries sustained, they claimed, during a recent fight with each other.

It became apparent that the girls were not telling the truth, and the detectives started looking at them more closely.

The girls told them that they had arrived at school on time on the morning of their mother's murder, and yet, when police checked CCTV footage it showed them at a gas station at 10 am that morning, proving that they didn't arrive at school in time, as they had claimed. Furthermore, surveillance footage from the school showed the girls arriving two and a half hours late.

If they had lied about that, what else had they lied about?

Their Arrest

With a lack of solid evidence, the twins were released to Della Frazier once more. Life returned to normal for the girls – the only thing out of the ordinary was their mother's funeral, which they attended with their boyfriends.

Haneef was disgusted by their behavior.

"I just knew it had to be the twins involved...and I couldn't believe that they weren't in jail. They showed up at the funeral with their boyfriends. These two twin girls don't have no kind of emotion...they sat by the casket, laughing and giggling...I couldn't believe it."

Sylvia witnessed the events, and how Haneef reacted.

"That's when her brother Haneef, he started to get upset...and he said 'y'all bitches are gonna tell me what y'all did to my sister?'"

As the weeks passed by with no further word from the police, the twins believed they were in the clear, but in the background, the investigation continued and police slowly but surely built their case against the Whitehead twins.

Forensic specialists had examined the bite marks on the girls' arms and hands, and compared them to a mould made from Nikki's teeth – they were a match.

In May 2010 Tas and Jas Whitehead were arrested and charged with murder, aggravated assault, and possession of a knife in commission of a crime.[9]

In January 2014, Tasmiyah received a 30-year sentence after pleading guilty to voluntary manslaughter, and one month later Jasmiyah received the same sentence after also pleading guilty.

The girls were sent to separate prisons – Tas is incarcerated in Pulaski State Prison, and Jas is in Arrendale State Prison, both of which are in Georgia.[10]

Nikki wanted the best for herself and, more importantly, for her two girls. Now, she is dead, and her precious girls will be middle-aged before they are released. It was not the life, or the death, she had wanted for any of them.

CONTRACT KILLER : THE TRUE STORY OF TERESA LEWIS

CHELSEA CROSS

Teresa Lewis:

Mastermind of Murder or Following Orders

A death sentence always causes a stir across the United States. It is used rarely and for good reason, but a majority of states have valid death penalty statutes. In 2016 alone there were 20 cases of the death penalty being used, and there have been more than 1,400 cases since the penalty was reinstated nationwide in 1976. Although that seems like a high number, there were more than 14,000 murders in just 2013. It should be noted that the average number of murders per year is dropping at a steady pace, however. Taking these numbers into account, approximately 0.14% of murders end in a conviction that results in the death penalty, which certainly makes the sentence a rare one. On top of that, it is even rarer that another country weighs in on a death penalty case, but when it comes to the circumstances of Teresa Wilson Bean Lewis that is exactly what happened. Both Amnesty International and the leader of Iran cried foul about the case, both for very different reasons.

Teresa is a somewhat tragic figure in her own right. She was diagnosed with substance dependencies, lower than average IQ, and at least one mental illness. It is contentious whether or not she was coerced into committing adultery with two men and then hiring them to kill her husband and one of her son-in-laws, but the fact remains that three people are now dead: Teresa, her husband Julian, and his son Charles. The loved ones who were left in the wake of this unfortunate and painful event have truly experienced something awful. When it comes to the death penalty, there is one consequence that goes unnoticed at first, but is felt more strongly as time goes on. There is no way to go back to the convicted murderer later and ask them more about why they did what they did. It is true that these questions can be asked before they are killed by the state, however, stories change as remorse strengthens. Psychiatric and psychological treatments advance over time, and sometimes evidence revisited gives us the window into the situation that we had missed at the time of the crime.

Whether Teresa deserved to die is controversial. There are many reasons that a court might lighten or strengthen a sentence. Teresa's supporters contend that her lower IQ should have reduced the severity of her sentence, while they also suggest that the court worsened the sentence because of her gender. Opponents point out that she orchestrated the deaths of her husband and son by her own confession, and for that reason alone she deserved death as is merited by the law of Virginia state. Regardless of which side holds the most weight, it is important for us to understand who Teresa was, why she committed such a terrible crime, and how we as a society can prevent crimes like hers from happening in the future.

Teresa Wilson of Danville, Virginia

Danville is a little city in Virginia with a quaint downtown area. It has a heritage properties vibe with lots of older, but well maintained, buildings. There seems to be an emphasis on greenery and the people take pride in their gorgeous rivers and bridges. It is here, in poverty, that Teresa Wilson was born in 1969. Her parents both worked in the local textile mill, and the family attended church regularly. Having some talent and passion for singing, Teresa sang in the church when she was young. When she was 16, she gave up attending school and instead got married to a man that she had met in the church that had been the source of pride in her life. The couple had one daughter whom they named Christie Lynn Bean, and divorced shortly after. It was at about that time that Teresa, now a Bean, reportedly turned to alcohol and painkiller in order to self medicate for mental illnesses that were undiagnosed. Her ex-husband's mother has been quoted as saying that Teresa was "not right" since then, which is a description that has followed her.

Teresa is not described as being an intelligent person, and due to her unfinished education, she struggled to find meaningful work.

After her divorce, she bounced around between low paying and underwhelming employment. Eventually, in the year 2000, she wound up at the Dan River textile mill and worked under a supervisor named Julian Clifton Lewis, Jr., who became her second husband. Julian Lewis had three children of his own, Jason, Charles, and Kathy. Charles was a reservist with the army of the United States. By June of 2000, Teresa and Julian were living together, and were married by the end of the summer. It is unclear how the relationship between Teresa and her three step-children was, and how Julian treated Teresa's daughter Christie, who would have been about 15 at the time, but soon all of their lives were about to drastically change.

A year later in December 2001, Julian's oldest son Jason Clifton Lewis, was killed in a car accident. His death was swift and unexpected, and brought with it a life insurance payout of $200,000. Although none of the family could have suspected it, the groundwork was laid for an even bigger tragedy. With the insurance money, Julian purchased a manufactured home along with a five acre parcel of land. Likely he was hoping to distract himself from his son's death as well as providing for his family in the future by ensuring that they had shelter no matter what happened. Slightly less than a year later in August 2002, Julian's youngest son Charles was preparing to leave for his first tour in Iraq as a member of the United States Army Reserve. In order to do so, he purchased a life insurance policy of $250,000 and denoted his father as the primary beneficiary. Although she had been his step mother for less than two years at that time, Charles made Teresa his second beneficiary, which was a mistake that cost him his life.

Teresa Lewis and a Contract for Murder

When Teresa met the killers of her son-in-law and husband at a Wal-Mart in the autumn of 2002, it would be great to know what exactly transpired. 21-year-old Matthew Jessee Shallenberger later wrote that "Teresa was in love with me. She was very eager to please me. She was also not very smart." It is likely that Shallenberger used Teresa's attraction to him in an attempt to get Charles's life insurance money. In a small town like Danville, word gets around when a resident signs up for the military and is about to get deployed. It is likely than many people living in the area knew about the life insurance policy. In October, when Charles returned home from an elite training program in Maryland for a visit, this news was spread around as well. At this point, Teresa was already embroiled in her secret plot (or Shallenberger's) and was also continuing a sexual relationship with him and his friend and fellow murderer 19-year-old Rodney Lamont Fuller. In late October, Teresa paid the young men $1,200 to purchase the appropriate amount of weapons and ammunition to be able to kill both Charles and her husband Julian.

Shallenberger and Fuller first attempted to kill Julian while out on the road. Either their attempt went completely unnoticed, or it wasn't reported to the police, because when it failed, Matthew and Rodney had only to wait for their second chance. Teresa left the door unlocked to their home and waited in her room during the second murder attempt. Shallenberger and Fuller sneaked into the home on October 30th late into the evening. Shallenberger slipped into Julian's room and shot him at least three times, decided he was dead, and left the room. Fuller was tasked with Charles: he used a shotgun to bring down the reservist, and then repeatedly shot him when he released that the other young man had not yet died. Once the ringing of the shots wound down, Teresa located her late husband's wallet and divided up the $300 within among her two accomplices. The men then left the premises and disappeared into the night. There is no indication of where Julian's surviving child, Kathy, was that night. After 45 quiet minutes passed, Teresa finally called the authorities. In the other room, Julian was still alive and bleeding out. Had she called the emergency services sooner, he might have lived, but as it is you don't hire someone to kill your family and then try to save them. The sheriff's deputies arrived on the scene shortly after her call and started to attend to Julian, which is when Teresa's husband said his last words: "My wife knows who done this to me." Teresa later tried to claim that men unbeknownst to her invaded the home and killed her family members. She would only be caught in her lie when she makes her first mistake.

From the outset, Teresa didn't have a long term plan of evading arrest. She probably believed that she wouldn't be caught. Almost immediately after her husband's death, she tried to withdraw $50,000 using a cheque she forged with his signature, which of course alerted the sheriff. During that first week, it was later proven that she had been trying to amass her husband and son-in-law's properties and estate before they had even been put into the ground. Due to the mounting evidence, she promptly confessed upon her arrest, and began working with the investigators, who set their sights on gathering evidence against Shallenberger and Fuller. However, her full cooperation would not save her life.

Teresa, in the Justice System

From the time she was arrested until the time she was executed, her trial garnered more and more attention throughout the United States and the world. She had three separate psychological evaluations by forensic psychiatrists. One of them, Barbara G. Haskins, was court appointed and board-certified, and she had this to say about Teresa: "Cognitive testing showed a Full Scale IQ of 72. [Her] Verbal IQ was 70, and Performance IQ was 79." Backing that up, Teresa's lawyer was quoted as saying that Teresa was "not mentally retarded, but she is very, very close to it." As mentioned earlier, Teresa had a painkiller addiction, alcoholism, and dependent personality disorder. She should have had a chance of being found unfit for trial, but the Attorney General of Virginia, Ken Cuccinelli, seemed to hold something extra against her: "the brutal nature of the crimes themselves as well as Lewis' callous, manipulating, adulterous, greedy, egregious behavior" had more than justified her death sentence. Her judge at the time also weighed in with Cuccinelli, saying that Teresa's worst actions had been the "cold blooded, pitiless slaying of two men, horrible and inhumane." He noted that she hadn't pulled the trigger, but that her aim for financial gain was clear by her rifling through her dying husband's wallet for cash.

Under Virginia law, the death penalty is the rule for sentencing someone who has committed more than one murder in under three years. Teresa's daughter received a five year sentence that she served, because she apparently knew about the plot and didn't report it, but the details on that part of the story are weak. Her partners in crime received mere life sentences, despite the fact that they were the ones who actually killed the two men, and the judge presiding over the case stated that Teresa was undoubtedly "the head of serpent." However, he decided that Fuller and Shallenberger deserved the same sentence, regardless of any other mitigating or aggravating factor in an effort to be fair. Many have since disagreed, including famous crime writer John Grisham, who said of the case: "As between Mrs. Lewis and Shallenberger, Shallenberger was definitely the one in charge of things, not Mrs. Lewis." Shallenberger killed himself in 2006, shortly after confessing, more or less, to using Teresa in the creation of the murder plot in order to gain the life insurance money. In a letter to an ex-girlfriend, Shallenberger wrote that he had dreamed of becoming a drug dealer in New York, and would have tricked Teresa out of the money in order to do so.

Grisham also wrote: "Why did the triggermen get life without parole while Lewis received a sentence of death? Ostensibly, it is because she was the ringleader and thus more culpable. But what could make a killer more culpable than repeatedly shooting a sleeping victim?" Besides John Grisham, there were approximately 7,300 appeals for clemency sent on behalf of Teresa to Bob McDonnell, who at the time was the Virginia governor. There were many people who were interested in keeping Lewis alive, but all of the appeals and statements were ignored. McDonnell made the decision not to grant her a stay of execution, and had this to say about it: "Having carefully reviewed the petition for clemency, the judicial opinions in this case, and other relevant materials, I find no compelling reason to set aside the sentence that was imposed by the Circuit Court and affirmed by all reviewing courts." There were, however, at least two Supreme Court judges that would have voted to grant her a stay of execution. As much as her supporters were biased in her favour, McDonnell seems to have been biased in the opposite direction as he has supported measures to extend the reach of the death penalty during his career.

Teresa, for her part, at least acted remorseful. In the appeals for clemency, her supporters wrote that "Lewis is deeply remorseful and has been a model prisoner, helping fellow female inmates cope with their circumstances." Speaking on her own behalf, Teresa stated that "I just want the governor to know that I am so sorry, deeply from my heart. And if I could take it back, I would, in a minute ... I just wish I could take it back. And I'm sorry for all the people that I've hurt in the process." At this point in time, Teresa was noticeably tense and frightened at the end of her life. There were reports that her jaw was clenched before she received the injection. Regardless of that, she managed to hold herself together while in the Fluvanna Correctional Center for Women in Troy, Virginia, although waiting for death and knowing it will inevitably come to you on a preplanned date is a difficult thing to live with. Near the end, she sang praises and hymns, likely trying to relive the days when she sang for her church. But one has to ask: what was this woman with low IQ doing on death row, anyway?

When Teresa was first cooperating with law enforcement and gaining them the information that they needed to make three more convictions, she led them straight to Shallenberger. At that time, her lawyers told her to plead guilty due to the overwhelming evidence against her. Reportedly, they gave this advice because they thought that, in front of a judge, Teresa would see leniency. Her judge in particular had never before handed down the death penalty, and because of this her attorneys felt this was her safest route. However, the judge was quick to sentence her to death, and in doing so, he did follow the word of the law closely. As was stated previously, the law in Virginia is two or more murders in three or less years means that the culprit will receive the death penalty. Did Teresa's lawyers not know that, were they poor gamblers, or did they feel that Teresa was not a person worth saving? It is impossible to do more than just speculate, but there was a mishandling a justice. Regardless of the fact that Teresa did plot a heinous action, as a criminal she still deserved to be protected legally. And again, it is important to remember that she did not pull the trigger, and that Shallenberger had an IQ of 113, which is in the high average range. Shallenberger also killed himself: was it from guilt, or was the life sentence too overwhelming for him? This was a man who killed another in cold blood for a woman he barely knew—and probably to get the insurance money.

Teresa spent her last days on death row at the Fluvanna Correctional Center while singing and trying to make the lives of others better. She wrote to her two blood-related children and was able to meet with them as well as her spiritual adviser before she was killed. During an interview, she tried to reach out to Kathy, who for good reason had not come to visit her, by telling the interviewer "I wish I could give Kathy the world and take away her hurt. I can't even imagine the pain she's been going through all these years." For her last meal, she choose two fried chicken breasts, sweet peas with butter, a Dr Pepper and German chocolate cake for dessert, which is an albeit humble but delicious sounding meal. For her last words, she said "I just want Kathy [her step-daughter] to know that I love you, and I'm very sorry." After that, she was killed by lethal injection of several toxic substances at the Greensville Correctional Center in Jarratt. Kathy, for her part, had said she would be there, but as an affected family member, she had been in a private viewing room. No one knows for sure whether or not she had actually been there, and the guards did not reveal her presence to Teresa. Kathy had told reporters earlier that "we just went to visit" her father and brother's graves with her children, because "that's the last place that I saw them." The last woman executed by Virginia had been killed by the electric chair back in 1912. As mentioned above, the death penalty is not often handed out lightly. It is possible that the judge who gave her the sentence initially assumed that her case would act as a deterrence against the rise in violent crimes committed by women, but there is no available statistical evidence that proves that lethal injection has ever worked as a criminal deterrent.

Right up to her death and afterwards, there were people who tried to use her death for their own purposes. Her lawyer James Rocap III said this about her sentence: "A good and decent person is about to lose her life because of a system that is broken ... it is grossly unfair to impose the death sentence on her while Shallenberger and Fuller received life." And about the weeks leading up to her death, Rocap said: "We thought that we were supposed to be helping her, while she was actually helping us." As her attorney, Rocap might have felt impassioned to say that about a woman who did, in whatever manner, see to it that her husband and son lost their lives. By this, Rocap is referring to the way in which Teresa carried herself and calmly addressed those who fought every inch of the way for her not to die. After her death, Rocap made some final comments about her: "Tonight the machinery of death in Virginia extinguished the childlike and loving spirit of Teresa Lewis." The spokesperson and executive director of Amnesty International, Larry Cox, one of the many foreign bodies to weigh in on the case, was quoted as saying: "Proceeding with this execution would come dangerously close to violating the U.S. Constitution, which prohibits capital punishment for those with 'mental retardation'—a precedent established thanks to Atkins v. Virginia." It is worthwhile to point out that Amnesty International opposes the death penalty in all circumstances around the world, and therefore is plenty biased towards people keeping their lives.

Even parts of the European Union tried to sway the case by asking McDonnell to downgrade her sentence to a life behind bars. Other groups who were advocating on Teresa's behalf included the Virginia Catholic Conference, the ARC of Virginia, and the Virginia Conference of the United Methodist Church. On top of Rocap and Cox both speaking out against the death penalty, so too did the leader of a country that permits the stoning of adulterers: President Mahmoud Ahmadinejad of Iran. He used the case to try and show that the global media's attention on a stoning case in his country was unwarranted because of what the United States did to Teresa Lewis. Of course, there is no comparison between lethal injection for double homicide and stoning for possible adultery. While the victim of the Iranian justice system died screaming and begging for her life as stone after stone hit her, Teresa's feet reportedly bobbed when the chemicals entered her body, and a guard lightly touched her shoulder to try and offer comfort while she passed away.

The Death Penalty and Teresa Lewis

Whether or not a person believes that the death penalty is ever warranted, and whether or not they think it was appropriate in Teresa's case, a woman is dead at the hands of Virginia state, and another two women are the sole survivors of their blended family. Whenever possible, it is crucial to understand the impacts that a crime has on the survivors. It is they who have to live with what happened. In this case, Teresa's daughter Christie had been sentenced for 5 years in prison, which leaves the only innocent party left alive: Kathy. Teresa apologized to Kathy before she was killed, but there is no record of how Kathy was feeling as her step-mother and the murderer of her father was put to death. Although it might have been out of respect for her privacy and mental health, it would have been beneficial for the full story had reporters gained access to Kathy's testimony. Reportedly, she has kept a scrapbook with every bit of detail from the case, and attended the execution to better honor her deceased family members.

Some commentators have wondered about a potential gender bias in these particular court hearings. Violent crimes by women are still rare when compared to the rates committed by men, and the amount of death row prisoners who are women is approximately 2% of all death row inmates. Teresa didn't pull the trigger and, potentially, she might not have been the mastermind, but her biography on a murderpedia website lists that her method of murder had been a shotgun. It is well known that her method of murder had been leaving the back door unlatched and allowing the killers to have access to her home. She stood idly by while her supposed loved ones were slain, but she did not shoot them herself. Her sexual conduct has also factored into the case in a way that would not be the case had she been a man, which is curious. Advocate Dahlia Lithwick writes: "It seems clear in hindsight that both her death sentence and her clemency petition contain gender assumptions that the criminal justice system does not spell out explicitly. She was sentenced harshly because she used sexuality and adultery to mastermind a murder plot against loved ones, and she seeks a reprieve from death because her sexuality made her a victim in uniquely female ways." However, by following the letter of the law and sentencing her to death for two murders in under three years, the judge was treating her the way in which he should treat any murderer of any gender. If anything, it could be argued that the sheer amount of publicity that her case garnered is simply because she was a woman.

In the end, the hymn singing murderer was killed by the state of Virginia, her main co-conspirator had killed himself, and Fuller is still serving out his days behind bars. Hopefully Kathy, Julian's daughter and Teresa's step-daughter, has been able to find peace after the death of her father's killer.

I HATE MONDAYS : THE TRUE STORY OF SCHOOL SHOOTER BRENDA SPENCER

DARLA PUGH

In 1979, a five-feet-one-inch, eighty-pound sixteen-year-old girl would become the first school shooter in United States history. Brenda Spencer would open fire on Cleveland Elementary School, wounding nine children and killing two adults. Her assault would be the first of many school shootings across the nation, most notably Columbine and Sandy Hook.

The media and public began looking for answers as to why someone would commit such a horrid act. The response from Brenda was callous and flippant.

She hated Mondays.

But there had to be more to the story than that. Monsters are not born, they're made.

This is how the monster was created.

EARLY LIFE

Brenda Spencer was born to Wally and Dot Spencer in 1963. She was the youngest of three children, having a brother named Scott and a sister named Teresa. Despite being raised in a sunny San Diego locale, her family resembled something you would expect in a home of inbred hillbillies. Her saw-toothed father worshiped guns, allegedly committed incest and later married a minor.

Brenda's mother, however, would describe the home as a happy one before she initiated a divorce.

"He (Wally) was fooling around with other women," Dot Spencer said. "And he came home one night and asked me if he could leave for a year and if I'd let him come back. He'd already rented an apartment somewhere. I just laughed jend a few days later I filed for divorce."

"That was just a rumor (his fooling around)," Wally said. "It was not true."

The divorce would hit Brenda hard. In her early childhood photos, she looked to be a happy child. Tiny but smiling in every picture like a normal kid. She enjoyed playing with her rabbit and spending time with her siblings.

"She (Brenda) was very active," Dot said. "She was always happy and a good child. Well-behaved. Never had any problems at school."

"After my parents got divorced it was like the latchkey kids," Brenda said. "It was like complete neglect."

Scott and Teresa opted to live with her father as in the 1970s era the court system allowed the children to have a say in picking the parent they wanted to live with.

Dot would lose custody of all the children, Brenda included.

"It (their custody battle) when the court system was swaying back and forth and he got the two older ones, they wanted to stay with him. And so they didn't want to split up the three so he naturally got Brenda."

"I went to court and I fought for custody," Wally said. "I loved my kids. I wanted to keep them, to raise them myself."

Dot alleged, however, that Wally wanted custody because he was too mean to pay child support.

The divorce would be the catalyst that would send Brenda's life into a tailspin. She became upset easily and felt invisible because her mother "was never around."

Brenda would claim that she would hardly ever see her mother and that when she did, her mother was indifferent to her presence.

"Sometimes I would stop by her house," Brenda said. "But she didn't seem to care to see us."

"That's not true," Dot said. "I'd see her once a week and then she'd come over and spend part of the weekend with me. I'd come home from work and she'd be sitting at the door waiting for me to come home. So we'd talk and what have you."

ABUSE...

Wally Spencer was a Navy veteran and a hunting enthusiast. He passed down his love for guns to Brenda, training her in marksmanship.

"She said she and her father had enough ammunition in the house for a small army," one classmate said. "Most of the boys and girls don't like her and won't go over to her house."

Wally worked as an audio-visual tech for San Diego State University. He had a steady job but for whatever reason, Wally elected to eke out a bleak existence. The furniture inside the home was sparse and allegedly they both shared the one sleeping mattress on the living room floor.

"I'd call him (Brenda's father) a loner," Dot said. "He didn't want to go to football games or baseball games. He'd just as soon stay home."

"The dad was a bitter man who hated the world," Brenda's attorney, Michael McGlinn said. "Her mother became a stone herself. You know, it was like, she never went out of her way to go over and see the kids, to have a relationship with Brenda so it was like a very cold, sterile environment in both places."

Brenda would later claim that she was both sexually and physically abused by her father which would be adamantly denied by Wally.

"I remember being hit in the face a lot," Brenda said. "Being hit in the ribs. Being yelled at, called names. I remember him coming home from work and being mad and smacking me in the head. And on different nights, he would just almost rape me. It was like that. Like he did. Like he would touch me inappropriately. I don't know how to say it."

Brenda would be asked as to why she never revealed this during his counseling sessions she would lie and say that she did, in fact, tell them about her incest but was ignored. During a later parole hearing, Brenda would claim to have been sodomized by her father.

"That never happened," Wally said. "I'll take a lie detector on that. That never happened."

During an interview with September Films, however, Wally came across as less convincing than his daughter when queried about the sexual abuse. He was asked if he ever molested his daughter and he raised his eyes in shock, looking like a bad actor.

"I don't have enough information to comment on the character of her father," District Attorney Richard Sachs said. "The only information I have is that she felt neglected by him and had accused him of sexual molest and forcing her to share a bedroom with him or bed with him. I don't know whether or not those allegations are founded or not. These are just things she (Brenda) has said."

"I had suspicions (of sexual molestations)," Dot said. "But she would never really tell me. The way she would be acting, very evasive if I asked her anything. It just wasn't her. I knew something was wrong."

HIGH SCHOOL...

Brenda began taking drugs in her high school years and became a truant. She turned to petty theft and shoplifting, staying home from school to watch any violent movie playing on television. She particularly enjoyed movies that featured cops being shot as she hated authority figures. Furthering her alienation, Brenda stated that she was "gay from birth."

Now a freckle-faced, red-haired girl who was impossibly thin, Brenda was noticeably different from the rest of her peers at Patrick Henry High School. She fell during a bike accident in her childhood and later tests would reveal that she had an injury to the front temporal lobe of her brain.

"This type of brain injury isn't uncommon among people who exhibit anti-social behavior," forensic psychologist Paula Orange said. "Brenda fell and hit her head. There are some instances where the injury is so severe that it changes a person's personality and outlook. Not making excuses for what she did but it could be part of the explanation of her personality changed to someone who craved violence."

She was described as "quiet" by most of her peers and some of her teachers thought her to be so introverted that they would inquire if she was awake.

But everyone thought she was harmless and no one thought she was capable of a mass shooting.

"She was never a violent person," Dot said. "I mean, (she) never beat up on the kids in the neighborhood or anything. Always very loving and caring and then all of a sudden she does something like this. It's hard to understand."

Despite her shy and reserved nature, Brenda did have some artistic ability. She was an avid photographer who had won a Human Society award for some of her shots.

Her passion wasn't shooting photos, however. It was shooting bullets.

"She wanted to blow a police officer's head off," said one classmate.

Brenda really wanted to kill a cop. She would have discussions with Brent, mapping out a plan where they would come up to a policeman sitting in a patrol car. Brenda would go to the passenger side window to distract him while her friend would shoot him from the driver side. She laughed as she talked about handcuffing him to the steering wheel then shooting him with his own gun. Another scenario would be for Brenda to lure him into a public restroom. She would throw eggs at his car and force him to follow her. Then once he set foot inside the bathroom she would kill him with an ax.

"She was always talking about guns," said another classmate. " Bragging about the guns her father had. She failed out of school last year (1978) and came back this year (1979. I didn't know her really well. I guess no one did."

Brenda would get expelled from high school due to her constant truancy. She was sent to a reform school who promptly informed her parents that Brenda was suicidal.

"Brenda was starting to have problems in school," Dot said. "They did send her to a special school. I had one interview with one of the people and they did say at that time that she was kind of suicidal."

Brenda's mother, however, never talked to Brenda about why she was suicidal.

"I figured her father would take care of her," Dot said. "You know, keep an eye on her."

Curiously, Wally would marry a seventeen-year-old cellmate of Brenda after she was jailed. Both parties refuse to reveal how the union came about.

"Sheila was her (Brenda's) cell mate in juvenile hall," Dot said. "She was released to go to a halfway house and she ran away from it. She went and got pregnant and they had to get married or go to jail."

The girl was younger than Brenda. People also marveled at how much she and Brenda looked alike.

"Her stepmother is younger than her," Dot said. "So they got married, had a daughter. Shortly after that Sheila left and left the daughter with Wally."

This revelation fueled the speculation that Wally may have been sexually abusing Brenda. When his daughter was incarcerated, he found a "replacement."

STARTING SMALL

The Spencers lived directly across from Cleveland Elementary School, less than one-hundred fifty feet away. Bored one weekend, Brenda would shoot up the windows at the school before breaking in and burglarizing one of the classrooms. She and a friend threw paint all over the classroom and overturned desks.

Brenda would be arrested and later released to her father's custody.

"She needs a lot of help," her probation officer said to the father. "I strongly urge you to admit her to a mental hospital. They'll take care of her, she's severely depressed."

"No," Wally said. "No hospitals."

Brenda would go on to have a "major fight" with her Dad. She absolutely refused to go to school because it was "boring."

Brenda's sister would later recall that she felt her father was too lenient with Brenda she would talk back to her dad. Brenda's sister did, however, say that her father made her "conform to the house rules." It became apparent, however, that when she challenged authority outside the home she would not get anything more than a slap on the wrist from her father.

BRING ON THE GUNS...

Brenda learned how to use a gun from her father and often bragged to other students on her prowess with weapons.

"She used to tell us how she went rabbit hunting in the mountains with a BB gun," said one friend.

"She'd shoot birds and cans," another classmate said "She had this long, straggly red hair. She was really scrawny, pretty crummy looking. She's a real little girl-real thin."

Deputy District Attorney Richard Sachs would later describe Brenda's appearance as "not like your typical sixteen-year-old. When you look into her eyes there is some type of emotional disturbance going on."

Brenda would become a truancy case, disdaining school and becoming a loner. She would skip school, take her BB gun to the local fields and shoot at small animals.

"She was different, that's for sure," a classmate said. "But she never really bothered anyone. You'd always see her walking around by herself at school."

With Brenda's anti-social behavior worsening, her father saw fit to give her a Ruger 10/22 semi-automatic .22 caliber rifle for Christmas in 1978. The rifle was equipped with a telescopic sight and 500 rounds of ammunition.

"He buys her a rifle with 500 rounds for Christmas," McGlinn said. "It's like 'Hello'!"

"I asked for a radio for Christmas," Brenda said. "And he bought me a gun."

"Why do you think he did that?" a reporter asked.

"I felt like he wanted me to kill myself."

Brenda immediately began practicing with the rifle. She placed all of her gun equipment in the garage, telling her friends that it would be her "fortress". She then dug a trench in the backyard and planned to use it as a "hideout tunnel".

"I'm going to do something to get on TV," Brenda told her friends as they saw the tunnel she dug in the backyard.

They were afraid to ask even though Brenda looked as if she wanted them to. She smirked at their fear and continued to dig the hole even deeper.

"I had failed in every other suicide attempt," Brenda later said. "I thought if I shot at the cops they would shoot me."

But her allegation of her father buying her a gun so that she cut kill herself is contradicted by her sister. According to Teresa, Brenda constantly badgered her father to buy her a rifle.

Strangely, her father would say later that Brenda never asked for a gun.

There was no record of any suicide attempts by Brenda yet she would talk about them in her letters after the shooting. She stated that the reason she could not kill herself was that she would "probably live, be a quadriplegic and be trapped even worse with Dad than I already was."

She wrote out a letter which explained why she did what she did.

"I want peace and see no other choice for myself."

Her father, however, found the letter and tore it to shreds.

DELUSIONS OF GRANDEUR...

Her best friend, Brent Fleming, recalled that day where Brenda had begun to dig the trench. He had accompanied her to shoot out the windows of the school and vandalizing it.

"Wait until Monday," Brenda told Brent. "Wait until you see what I'm going to do. It might even be big enough to make the news."

Brent recalled that Brenda's fantasies of being famous were not new.

"She stated on occasion that she would be famous," Fleming said.

The two hated all authority but with Brenda, it became the overriding theme of her life. Brent's mother recalled how they would sit around on the couch all day and complain about being hassled.

"They used to talk about what a rotten place the world was," Brent's mother said. "About how everybody hassles you. But nobody hassled them."

THE FATEFUL DAY

Brenda perched her rifle outside her bedroom window. She peered through the telescopic sights on her weapon and waited for the right moment.

Her heart began to race as the children stepped to the gates, arriving in groups of two or more. Brenda took a deep breath and squeezed the trigger.

Once she started, she couldn't stop.

January 29th, 1979 started as a normal day for Principal Burton Wragg. He stood in the front office, sipping from a cup of coffee while chatting with sixth-grade teacher Daryl Barnes.

The two then heard what they thought were a series of firecrackers going off outside.

Wragg went through the front door while Barnes went through the side.

Barnes turned the corner and found Wragg attending to a crying child on the ground. The principal then turned around and fall back into the bushes, blood on his chest.

Barnes grabbed as many children as he could, shoving them back into the front office.

"Call the police!" he screamed at the school secretary.

Running back outside, he rescued another child, hearing the shots ring out. He sprinted back to the office, looking back to see school custodian Mike Suchar coming to Wragg's aid with a blanket.

Suchar seemed unaware that there was sniper fire and was hit before Barnes could warn him.

"My God, I've been hit," Suchar said before falling to the ground.

A car full of children then drove up, equally unaware that a sniper was firing away.

"Get the car out of here!" Barnes screamed. "Get out!"

"It was a strange morning," Crystal Hardy, a surviving victim recalled. "It was just an eerie morning. There was frost on the grass. There was kind of a strange feeling."

"I remember walking to school by myself," Monique Selvig said. "I was about five feet from the sidewalk and then I heard firecrackers, the bullets that she was shooting go off. Then I turned around and faced directly across the street and got shot."

Her first shots wounded a couple of the children. Immediately taking action, the 53-year old Principal Wragg rushed over to protect the students, yelling at them to take cover inside.

"I looked out," Gaetana Payton, one of the schoolteachers said. "And the principal was flailing backward. And he had blood on his chest. And I thought 'Oh my gosh!'"

But another shot from Spencer hit Wragg and the Principal staggered to the ground. School custodian Michael Suchar rushed to the Principal's aid, trying desperately to drag him out of harm's way.

Brenda fired again, fatally wounding the heroic custodian.

The children scattered, screaming as Brenda fired away.

Robert Robb was one of the first police officers on the scene. He encountered a chaotic situation, children running and screaming. Two men on the ground bleeding.

Complete confusion and chaos.

"As we drew closer we could hear shooting," Robb said. "And as we arrived we could see a bunch of little school kids all huddled against the wall."

Robb exited his vehicle but was shot in the neck by Brenda.

"The bullet went in and it nicked my jugular vein," Robb said. "It bounced off my shoulder blade and lodged in my spine."

The spray of bullets would go on intermittently for the next fifteen minutes. Brenda would fire off a total of thirty rounds then barricaded herself inside her home. Police determined which house the gunfire was coming from and drove a garbage truck in front of Brenda's home to block her line of fire.

Authorities then began evacuating students out of the rear exit of the school. The children were then taken inside a school bus and driven to safety.

MEDIA COVERAGE AND CHAOS

A news reporter began calling homes in the immediate vicinity of the homes in the hope of contacting someone who could give him more detailed information.

He inadvertently dialed Brenda's number. The giggling sixteen-year-old admitted that she was the one responsible.

"I just started shooting," Brenda said. "That's it. I just did it for the fun of it."

"You may have killed three or four people," the reporter said.

"Is that all?" Brenda asked, her tone calm and matter-of-fact. "I have to go now. I shot a pig, I think and I want to shoot more.

Nine children would be wounded, one of whom was ten-year-old Crystal Hardy.

"I got shot and I was just waiting there," Crystal said. "Then I went to the nurse's office."

"The shot went through her wrist," Crystal's mother said. "Didn't hit the bone or anything. We're just praising the Lord."

"You're lucky," the reporter said.

"It was a very, very horrific event," Crystal said twenty-six years later. "My Mom just praised Jesus Christ because I was still alive. Certainly, it effected my life I mean it is something that traumatic would, of course, affect your life."

Nine-year-olds Monica Selvig and Christy Buell would be in critical condition. The bullet would exit through Monique's back, near her spine. Buell would be shot twice by Spencer, once in the stomach and her lower back.

Eight-year-old Mary Clark would be shot in the stomach as well, the bullet passing through.

"She (Mary) didn't tell anybody she was shot," a police officer said. "She just went back to her class. She was afraid to talk to anyone."

"I remember Crystal Hardy screaming," Selvig said. "Am I gonna die? Am I gonna die? Am I gonna die?"

THE STAND OFF

Police surrounded the Spencer home, shouting their demands through a bullhorn.

"I'll come out shooting," she said as police demanded that she surrender.

The SWAT (Special Weapons and Tactics) force arrived and staked out Brenda's home. They called her on the phone numerous times and she would simply hang up after a few tense words. Chester Thurston III, one of the primary police negotiators screamed through his bullhorn, ordering Brenda to surrender.

"I was irritating her like crazy," Thurston said. "I was squeaking the bullhorn. Basically raising all kinds of hell with her."

But Brenda knew what the protocol was for the SWAT teams. Her situation was playing out just like the ones she would watch on TV.

"She knew a lot about our operation from watching SWAT on TV," said SWAT member Mike Hendrikson. "She fantasized in the past about being a sniper."

The police would call back repeatedly and Brenda would alternate between being defiant and excited at the prospect that they would come and put her in handcuffs. Brenda wanted to get on television so her friends could see that she did "something big."

"Are there reporters outside?" Brenda asked.

"Brenda, you need to come out."

"Are there reporters outside?"

"Yes."

"And TV cameras?"

"Yes."

"Wow," she giggled.

The police realized that Brenda was home alone. They tried to appeal to her sense of family by asking about her parents.

"Do you have anything you want to say to your father?" the negotiator asked.

"Yeah," Brenda said. "Tell him to get screwed."

"How about your mother?"

"No. But I don't like her either."

After almost seven hours of back and forth, Brenda would get bored and surrender. Without warning, she stepped out of her home, placed her weapon down and gave herself up.

"I was a little pissed that the SWAT team didn't blow the whole house away," Robb said. "With her in it...I was shocked. To see this little girl, dressed up in what looked like army fatigues."

SWAT members would rush the home and find beer and whiskey bottles scattered on the floor. Brenda, however, did not appear to be intoxicated. She got into the police vehicle and was transported to the station, never saying one word until she addressed the media.

"I just started shooting," Brenda said. "That's it. I just did it for the fun of it. I just don't like Mondays. I did this because it's a way to cheer up the day. Nobody likes Mondays."

THE AFTERMATH...

Christy Buell would be hospitalized for a month after the shooting. She would then spend the next year and a half recovering physically. The mental aspect, however, would be a different story.

"There's no other way to say it," Buell said, her voice quivering with emotion. "I'll just never get over it."

Buell had lost her mother seven years earlier to leukemia and described her father's grief as "unimaginable." He had lost his wife and now faced the prospect of losing his daughter. Buell is also quick to remember the two men that were killed that day, Principal Burton Wragg and custodian Michael Suchar.

"The loss of two men that put their lives in danger to save children, that's the hardest part for me," Buell said. "The part no one will ever undo."

"I remember sitting watch TV that day," Principal Wragg's daughter Penny Buckley said. "And they are showing the same thing over and over again. Of course, it was everywhere, the news of my father (Principal Wragg) getting shot. And I remember sitting there, catching myself, anticipating Daddy getting home so I could tell him what happened."

Monica Selvig would get over physical aspect of the shooting but the mental trauma would always remain.

"She's evil looking," Selvig said years later after being shown a picture of Brenda. "I mean she's got these little glasses and those eyes. It is like something out of a horror flick. I mean I've never heard her talk but just she's eerie looking."

"I went to collect my Dad's things a couple days afterward," Buckley said. "And there was still blood on the sidewalk where he had died.

"It basically ended my career," Police Officer Robert Robb said. "It affected my ability to find a job. I mean I still dream about being a police officer and being out in the street. If I could I could go back to work tomorrow."

Brenda would be charged with two counts of murder and multiple counts of aggravated assault. Her trial had to be moved out of the San Diego area to Santa Ana in Orange County.

She did not find a sympathetic jury there, however. Brenda would be convicted on the murder charges and one count of assault.

Brenda would be sentenced to concurrent prison terms of twenty-five years to life (for murder) and forty-eight years (for assault with a deadly weapon).

Her "I don't like Mondays" comment would inspire a punk-rock song of the same name which was performed by the Bob Geldof and the Boomtown Rats. Geldof heard about what Brenda had done and then wrote the song in his hotel room.

"I tried to picture the girl," Geldof said. "I tried to visualize the scene: the police captains, the bullhorns, the playground, the parents.

The girl must be some sort of automaton. And I wrote, 'The silicon chip inside her head gets switched to overload.' And, of course, why was she doing it? 'Tell me why?' May she's right. Maybe there is absolutely no reason. But it seems the California ethos didn't allow for reasons and logic for doing anything. They just did it."

The song would become an enormous hit in Europe but Colombia records became fearful of litigation from victims. They withdrew the song from radio airplay in the US after only a week.

"I don't like the Boomtown Rats," Brenda said when asked about the song. "But I like the song because it makes me feel famous."

PAROLE?

During parole board hearings, Brenda would later claim to be under the influence of both drugs and alcohol during the shootings. She recalled the SWAT members coming into her home, thinking that they were "commandos storming my house."

She would also claim that she had shot the people in self-defense in her deluded mind.

"I was watching TV and started drinking," Brenda said. "Whiskey and taking pills with it and I was smoking marijuana with PCP. And I started hallucinating. And when I look out I saw commando guys in combat gear coming up. Basically, I think I was trying to get myself killed."

This claim was repudiated by the arrest record as she tested negative for both alcohol and drugs.

San Diego Deputy District Attorney Richard Sachs said that Brenda is still psychotic and opposed her parole application.

"When her girlfriend was released from jail," Sachs said "She (Brenda) burned the words 'courage' and pride in her arm like a tattoo (she used a hot paper clip). She's still subject to depression."

According to Brenda, however, the self-inflicted tattoos do not read 'courage' and 'pride'."

"It says unforgiven and alone," Brenda said, fighting back tears. "Unforgiven and alone."

Brenda as been open about her willingness to face the families of the people that she killed or wounded.

"They probably have questions," Brenda said. "It's not much, but it's the only thing I could do, answer some of their questions."

"I'm very sorry that I did it. I didn't have a right to do that to those people."

Brenda is now serving a 25-year-to-life sentence at the California Institute for Women in Frontera.

Her father remains her only visitor. He makes the five-hour round trip visit every Saturday from San Diego to Frontera.

"I don't feel responsible for what she did," Wally said. "But I still love her. She's my daughter and I still see her every Saturday if I can."

"I can't explain why she did it," Wally said. "I don't know."

Kathe Wragg, the widow of Burton Wragg, is a lot less lenient.

In her words, Brenda is "a pathetic, self-absorbed, bored, and uncaring thrill seeker" as her actions on January 29th, 1979 left innocent families devastated for decades after.

KILLER NURSE KIMBERLY SAENZ

JAMES FALCON

Kimberly Clark Saenz was a nurse. Almost ten years ago now, in 2008, she worked in a clinic called the DaVita Lufkin Dialysis Center. The clinic was- and still is- in Lufkin, a small blue collar city in East Texas of around 33,000 souls. But rather than care for her patients, she decided to kill. Because of a home life fraught with difficulties- she and her husband has fought, he had filed for divorce, and even taken out a restraining order against her- Kimberly's unrestrained and misdirected anger was taken out on her patients. And this was just the latest in a long list of healthcare jobs that Kimberly had held, after a spate of firings for various misdemeanours.

Even though she worked in a dialysis center, where there is normally little to cause complications and death, the number of patients dying on her watch alerted and disturbed other hospital staff. Even so, it took far too long for her managers and the authorities to find out what she had been doing. When, to their horror, they uncovered her crimes, Kimberly became national news.

Who was Kimberly Clark Saenz?

Kimberly hadn't had the best start in life. She was born Kimberly Clark Fowler in Fall River, Massachusetts in 1973. After an uneventful childhood during which she moved away from Massachusetts to Texas, she dropped out of high school in her senior year after falling pregnant. Kimberly and her husband would go on to have two children together, but Kimberly struggled with addiction and the strains this put on her home life.

She suffered from substance abuse problems, which proved to be a drain on the family finances; it was also enough to convince her to steal, which she did time and time again from her various employers. According to witness testimony at her trial, Lufkin law enforcement told the court that she had been arrested multiple times for intoxication and criminal trespass after domestic disturbances with her husband, Kevin Mark Saenz. She was clearly unhappy with the direction in which her life was heading.

Before taking the nursing position that would prove to be her last, Kimberly had been fired from four similar jobs in the recent past. Each time had been because she was caught stealing medication in her handbag once her shift was over. What is worse is that she lied each time to her prospective employer, claiming that she had no criminal history to speak of, even though when she applied for her final care work position she had actually been on bail. In this way it would be fair to say that the deaths Kimberly caused were as much as anything because of a failure of oversight, and a failure to correctly check employees' criminal histories.

But in the end, it took a letter from a top fire official to actually get the matter investigated. The letter was sent anonymously, but complained of the highly unusual number of patients being transferred to hospital. The letter was sent in April 2008, and read 'In the last two weeks, we have transported 16 patients. This seems a little abnormal and disturbing to my med crews. Could these calls be investigated by you?'

Surveyors arrived within the next few days to try and get a handle on the situation. But if anything, this blew the case wide open: they realised that over the course of the preceding month, emergency crews had been called out a total of thirty times, seven of whom had cardiac problems, and four of whom died. To anybody unaware of the normal operation of a dialysis center, this may or may not have seemed excessive; but in comparison to the previous fifteen months before then, emergency services had only been required twice, according to the Texas Department of Health Services. Because of the strict quality controls involved in green lighting medical equipment and medicine for public use, all signs pointed to another cause: a person.

How was Kimberly caught?

Kimberly was eventually caught out because of her own brazen attitude to the crimes she committed. More of the details would come out once the case was brought to trial, but a number of eye witnesses had separately and independently told Kimberly's superiors that they had seen her poisoning the people she was supposed to care for. On the morning of April 28th, Kimberly arrived at work at 4:30am, only to be told that she was no longer on the rota to work as patient care technician- in charge of medication- she was to work as a simple patient monitor, who would check up on patients over the course of the day, and perform basic cleaning duties. According to her supervisor Amy Clinton, Kimberly's response was strange: she began crying, wiping away tears, and said that that particular job was beneath her. Amy had only been working at the DaVita clinic for a few days, and had been called in because of two recent and unusual deaths.

At 6am, the two witnesses were brought to the clinic- Lurlene Hamilton and Linda Hall. They were suffering with failing kidneys, and dialysis was not unusual for either of them; indeed, patients often undergo the treatment at least three times a week, and the procedure can take hours. There's little to do but sit, read, or talk to family or other patients. They were around 40 feet away from another two patients named Marva Rhone and Carolyn Risinger. They watched as Kimberly Saenz poured bleach from a jug into a cleaning bucket, and then as she drew up a small amount of the bleach into a syringe. This first concerned the witnesses because they felt that whatever the bleach was being used for, the bucket was most likely an unsanitary place to draw it from.

But what shocked them was what happened next. Kimberly approached the two patients, Rhone and Risinger, and injected the bleach into the feed lines of the dialysis machines that they were hooked up to. Fortunately, neither went into cardiac arrest, presumably because Kimberly did not or could not inject enough bleach into the system. But the eyewitness testimony of Hamilton and Hall was proven correct during later analysis, which found bleach in Rhone's dialysis line. Bleach, of course, has a terrible effect on the body; it easily eats through tissue and when injected into the blood can cause blood cells to burst. Because of the overload of potassium this can cause in the blood stream, cardiac arrest often immediately ensues. That being said, bleach is generally eliminated from the body quite quickly, and if the victim survives, they very rarely suffer any further lasting effects.

A key point to understand is that bleach is regularly used in dialysis clinics across the country. First, of course, for general cleaning of the floors and walls: blood is easily spilled and contamination is a major risk. But in addition, bleach is the most common cleaning fluid used to clear dialysis lines after being used. As such, there are strict guidelines over its use: it should be clear that injecting it into the dialysis lines while still in use by patients is against those guidelines!

In addition to this eyewitness testimony, after just a brief analysis of the rota, one of the inspectors found that Kimberly had been working on a staggering 84% of the shifts when a patient suffered either chest pain or cardiac arrest. She had been working there in an entry level position for eight months up until that point, and this bizarre discrepancy was enough to get Kimberly fired in April 2008.

On the same night as those final attacks, Lufkin Police officer of thirteen years Bradley Baker was called out to Mark Kevin Saenz's home at around 8:30pm. The couple had split not long ago. Baker described what happened next during his testimony at trial: "Ms. Saenz was banging on the door of the house. Her eyes were glassy and she was having trouble answering questions." Baker issued a criminal trespass warrant to Kimberly, and upon talking to her further she admitted that she was taking Cymbalta and drinking. She was arrested for public intoxication, and at this point, the police knew nothing of what she had done earlier that day at the dialysis clinic.

Kimberly on trial

When Kimberly was brought to trial, she faced five separate murder charges over the deaths of Clara Strange, Thelma Metcalf, Garlin Kelley, Cora Bryant and Opal Few. She was accused of having killed them through poisoning them with sodium hypochlorite- better known to us as bleach- through injecting it into their dialysis lines. In fact, two eyewitnesses claimed that she had attacked two different patients on the date of April 28th, 2008. Her attorneys argued that she had been set up: she was a scapegoat for the DaVita clinic, which had been failing its patients long before the spate of deaths that April in 2008.

The two witnesses, Linda Hall and Leraline Hamilton, claimed that those two patients- Marva Rhone and Carolyn Risinger- had been injected with bleach that day. In addition, the Food and Drug Administration (FDA) prepared a report which confirmed that samples from a number of the victims had indeed tested positive for bleach, and while other samples were unclear, there was evidence that bleach "may have been present at one time." To come to that conclusion, they examined blood tubing, syringes and IV bags which had been used for the patients' dialysis.

The information about Saenz that came out during trial was shocking, and did nothing to dispel the idea that she should never have been allowed in a position of care. She had previously been fired from Woodland Heights hospital for stealing Demerol, which had been found in her handbag at the end of a shift. Very soon after having been fired from the DaVita clinic, she was suspended from the profession and her nursing licence was taken away. In between her firing and the trial, she worked as a receptionist without disclosing why she had been forced to find employment.

Kimberly refused to take the stand in her own defence, but her lawyers argued that she was a good woman who could never fathom killing another human being. 'Kimberly Saenz is a good nurse, a compassionate, a caring individual who assisted her patients and was well liked,' one of her defense attorneys, T. Ryan Deaton, told the court. And in a pre-recorded video message, Kimberly told the court that she felt 'railroaded' by the clinic; she had been the fall guy for the clinic, which desperately needed somebody to pin their failings on.

Her defense team argued that the marital issues and family strife she had been through prior to the murders had been overemphasised by the prosecution. To try and prove their point, they called upon an extensive number of character witnesses who each testified that Kimberly was not the woman she was made out to be in the press. If anything, she was a good woman, a caring woman who loved her family despite her struggles with addiction.

The first witness they called upon was Vernon Dean Warren, who had been dating Mark Saenz's mother at the time of the murders. He testified that he held no ill will against her at all, and that she was welcome to his home anytime. A friend of Kim's, Peggy Wells, also took to the stand to defend her friend. She had met Saenz in kindergarten, so had known her for well over thirty years. Peggy felt that Kimberly was no danger to either society or to her children.

Next up for the defence was Wendy Bryan, who had met Kimberly while she worked at Fleetwood Transportation, and where Kimberly had worked for several years. She told the packed courtroom that Kimberly had been a model employee, and that her personal troubles should not cloud anybody's mind about the person Kimberly really was. Asked about whether she felt that Kimberly was a good employee and a good person despite her personal issues, Wendy responded: "I would have absolutely hired her. Absolutely, without a doubt."

Another former employee of Fleetwood Transportation, Tonya Monlar, testified that Kimberly was "a very hard worker, very thorough." She even said that no matter what the outcome of the trial turned out to be, she would still keep in touch with Kimberly because she believed her to be a genuine and good person. "If I can visit, I'll visit. I'll write, and she's always in my prayers," she told the court. Yet another character witness was Barbara Allen, who had taught both Kim Saenz and her son. She told the court that Kimberly was a caring mother who had sacrificed her own schooling to go through with having her firstborn despite being so young. The local elementary school principal described how Kim was dedicated to her son: "When [he] was younger, he played baseball with my son. Kim was always there," said Karen Schumaker. And she described Kim's daughter as "a great kid".

Kimberly had sworn in an affidavit that she had no criminal record whatsoever, but a basic check revealed her extensive list of felonies: including the overuse and misuse of prescription drugs, general substance abuse problems, theft and violence. Prosecutors branded her defence a joke, calling it 'absolutely ridiculous'. They painted her as both a depressed and disgruntled employee, who on the testimony of her fellow nurses was always complaining about her patients, in particular those who required extensive care. They had even found evidence from her computer that she had searched for information on the Internet about bleach poisoning, whether bleach could poison a person through being injected into the blood, and whether bleach was traceable.

At one point in the trial, the victims of Kimberly's crimes were encouraged to speak and testify as to the misery she had caused. Thelma Metcalf's daughter told Kimberly: "You are nothing more than a psychopathic serial killer. I hope you burn in hell". The prosecution were also completely straightforward in their assessment of Kimberly's role and her obvious guilt: "The only days there were deaths in April, she was there," the attorney for the prosecution said. "Dialysis patients are sick, but every source of information we can find says it is very unusual for patients to die during dialysis treatment."

The attorney for the prosecution was Clyde Herrington. He believed that there were far more victims than those which were being discussed at the trial, an opinion based on the research of an epidemiologist at the Center for Disease Control and Prevention. That research categorically connected Saenz to the crimes, so it was a shame that Lufkin Police detectives were only able to find evidence from the two weeks prior to Kimberly being sacked. As such, there was nowhere near enough evidence to bring a successful case for those other victims; although given Kimberly's obvious guilt, and her modus operandi, it was plain to see that she had done far more damage than the few victims she was on trial for.

Kimberly's defense knew that she stood little chance of being found innocent of the charge of murder. So, rather than argue for her to be set free, they tried to have her charge of capital murder reduced to one of first degree murder- in other words, she would be in prison for life no matter what, but could avoid the death penalty. In summary, another of Kimberly's defense attorneys named Steve Taylor told the jury "She's never getting out no matter what you do... Society is protected. You will never see her again." Taylor also pointed out to the jury that Kimberly had been free during the period of the trial, and that prosecutors could not demonstrate that she had been a danger to the public.

To prove their point, the defense brought in Frank G. AuBuchon, a retired former employee of the Texas Department of Criminal Justice. Through him, the defense wanted to prove that just because they were pushing for something other than the death sentence, that Kimberly could never be a danger to the community again. Describing Kimberly's probable sentence, AuBuchon said: "It's a true life sentence. These people will die in custody." On the topic of what her life behind bars would be like, he said "You very quickly in prison the easiest way to do your time is to behave yourself. You get more privileges... Mind your own business. Don't tell anybody why you're there. Obey the rules." Finally, Frank Taylor told the court: "You will never see them again in society. They belong in another society now, the prison society."

On the other hand, during their summation, the prosecution did not specifically push for the death penalty. But they did remind the jury of Kimberly's criminal past, her issues with prescription drugs, and her propensity to lie to get what she wants. Just before the jurors retired to consider their verdict, Clyde Herrington told them: "I know you'll reach a verdict that's just and in accordance with the law," while showing them photos of the many victims who had suffered and died because of Kimberly and her actions. It was the prosecution that got what they wanted.

Kimberly was found guilty on March 31st, 2012, on the charge of capital murder, which covered each of the five murders. It was also clear that she had attacked, injured and killed far more patients than just those five. Just a few days afterwards, on April 2nd 2012, the jury sentenced Kimberly on behalf of Angelina County to life in prison with no hope of parole, and three separate twenty year sentences for aggravated assault. She remains in prison to this day.

What made Kimberly kill?

For anybody with even a passing knowledge of true crime, 'nurses who kill' are a recognisable and uniquely interesting subgroup of serial killers who continue to fascinate the American public. Genene Jones killed anywhere between six and sixty infants as a pediatric nurse in the '70s; Kristen Gilbert, 'the Angel of Death' killed four and tried to kill two more with epinephrine as a nurse in Massachusetts. Judy Buenoano, another nurse, was sentenced to die by electric chair for killing a string of previous husbands.

This isn't to suggest that there's something horrible about nurses! But the same trope is seen across the globe. Take Britain's Harold Shipman for instance: one of the UK's most infamous serial killers was a doctor, not a nurse, but killed at least 250 people over the course of decades. Each of these cases is tied to the others by the unique horror of killers who were supposed to care; murderers who were supposed to cure.

They are also linked by the fact that the underlying cause of all this misery and death is often inexplicable. Harold Shipman, for example, never expressed guilt or remorse. He maintained his innocence until his suicide in prison, as did his wife Primrose. As part of their case against Kimberly, the prosecution didn't actually have to prove her motive. But Clyde Herrington did speak to a registered nurse, one who had done extensive research into nurses and doctors who kill. But her research-which took in over a hundred killers- couldn't point to any unifying motive.

As Herrington put it to the jury, "Criminal behavior is something we've been trying to understand since Cain killed Abel. Only when the health care killer confesses do we know motive." But what Herrington claimed was that Kimberly had been driven to kill by her own troubles with both prescription drugs and her failing marriage. "From talking to some of the folks who worked with her, it sounded like her husband didn't want her to quit (DaVita)," Herrington continued. "She was depressed. She was frustrated, and I think she took those frustrations out on the patients."

How did Kimberly get away with her crimes for so long?

Kimberly Saenz's defense attorney, Ryan Deaton, claimed that the DaVita clinic was already plagued by malpractice and unusual deaths long before Kimberly started working there. Prior to the beginning of the trial, Deaton had fought hard for the jury to be able to see a report by the U.S. Department of Health and Human Services, which had been heavily critical of the DaVita clinic and its working practices. It had been ruled inadmissible by the state District Judge, Barry Bryan.

The report supposedly claimed that from December 1st 2007 until April 28th 2008, the clinic had overseen nineteen deaths, while over the entirety of 2007 there had been 25. Overall, this put the clinic above the state average, but only by seven percent.

But more importantly, the DaVita clinic was also accused within this report of shoddy record keeping that put patients at risk. Over the period between September 1st 2007 and April 26th 2008, 102 patients from the DaVita clinic had been transported to a local hospital either during or immediately after their dialysis treatment. Of these 102 patients, 68 cases had not been fully written up with a complete adverse occurrence report. So even though it was undoubtedly Kimberly who killed those people- there was no other way for bleach to make its way into the dialysis machines, and she was seen by two separate eyewitnesses with the syringe filled with bleach in her hand- the shoddy record keeping allowed an environment in which somebody who wanted to do what Kimberly did could get away with it.

The report summarised its findings with a damaging conclusion on the DaVita clinic and the ability of its staff. Their findings suggested that the DaVita clinic and its staff "did not demonstrate competence in monitoring patients during treatment alerting nurses or physicians of changes to a patient's condition and following the physician's orders for the dialysis treatment." In response a spokesman for the DaVita clinic, Vince Hancock, said that the company's actions did not lead to any deaths in April 2008, and that the court case proved it. "We hope that healing can start to occur for families of victims and for our teammates who also have been victimized by the murderous acts of Kim Saenz," he told the press.

Kimberly's retrial

Unbelievably, Kimberly and her defense lawyers felt that she stood a chance of winning an appeal, and they immediately sought leave to fight their case in the Court of Appeals. But the judgment of her first trial was upheld in a decision issued in August 2015. "Although both the jury charge and argument of counsel weigh in favor of egregious harm, we conclude the state of the evidence and the record as a whole substantially support a finding of guilt in regard to each of the capital murder victims," the opinion stated. "Accordingly, we hold the record does not establish egregious harm, and we affirm the trial courts judgment."

One of the central points of the appeal was that the Angelina County district court had allowed the jury to find her guilty, even though they could not unanimously agree on which exact patients had been killed by Kimberly; the judge had felt it to be obvious enough that she had killed at least some of the patients who had died, due to circumstantial evidence and eyewitness accounts.

The court dismissed each of the 21 issues which Saenz put before them, and had initially issued their ruling on January 22nd, 2014, but this ruling was itself overruled in December of that same year by the Texas Court of Criminal Appeals. The appeal was then sent back to the Fourth Court of Appeals, but she was again unsuccessful. Herrington, the original attorney for the prosecution, claimed that she would have appealed no matter what the grounds, but he didn't think she would be very successful. "Kim Saenz is sentenced to a life without parole," Herrington said. "She has absolutely no reason to continue to appeal as long as the possibility even exists."

Kimberly remains in prison to this day, universally considered guilty of the crimes she was sentenced to. She has no chance of parole; the only downside is that we may never know exactly what motivated her to kill.

DARLA PUGH

At first glance, Michelle Theer looked like the stereotypical bored housewife. She married an Air Force captain who was deployed on assignment for long periods of time. Her days were spent alone and idle.

And you know what they say about idle hands.

Michelle felt unfulfilled in her marriage and didn't so much want out, she wanted something more. Attractive with long brown hair and arched eyebrows, Michelle did not have any problems attracting members of the opposite sex. She needed something discreet, however, something that would simply titillate her fantasies and relief the boredom that she would suffer during the long absences of her husband.

So she turned to the Internet.

It started innocently at first. A few keystrokes of flirtatious messages. Some a bit racier than others, but where was the harm? She was hiding behind a computer monitor. It isn't cheating if there is no face to face, Michelle thought.

Then she came across the profile of John Diamond. His pictures showed him to be a tall and muscular man, a special forces soldier that made Michelle's heart skip a beat.

Or maybe she saw him as the perfect foil. The perfect fall guy to get rid of her husband.

Their flirtations started innocently enough. Then the messages got racier and racier until they both felt the need to satiate their fantasies for one another.

Those fantasies led to sex.

Then murder.

Frank Theer, better known as "Marty", was a quiet and reserved young man. In high school, his friends introduced him to what they believed what be his perfect match.

Michelle Forcier.

Michelle was outgoing, bubbly and only sixteen when she met Marty who was a year older. Her friends believed that Michelle's extroverted personality could be a counterweight to Marty's introverted nature. Marty had originally intended to become an astronaut, his ambition and intelligence made him an attractive catch to Michelle. They were both the product of military families, both moving a lot as children so they had a kinship there. Both were ambitious and had concrete plans for the future. Marty would join the Air Force. Michelle would join the reserves and serve in the Gulf War.

"Michelle had ambition," forensic psychologist Paula Orange said. "She wanted status and respect. But she grew up in a military family and succumbed to the tribalism and social pressures that existed in that kind of environment. You grow up, get married and have kids. Michelle probably had mixed feelings about that. She wanted to do her own thing. So, in essence, she was living a double life from the get-go. She was doing the expected thing of getting married but on the side she was the libertine, drinking heavily and having extra-marital affairs."

The couple would maintain their long-distance relationship for four years until Michelle was assigned to the Persian Gulf War in 1991. Thinking that their courtship had lasted long enough, Marty asked Michelle to marry him.

Michelle, at twenty years old, said yes to the other man she had known up until that point.

Their wedding video would show the couple to be a happy one. They kissed for the cameras and fed each other wedding cake.

"We did everything together," Michelle said. "He treated me really well. I just thought we had the perfect relationship. We were best friends."

The couple would remain married for six years as Marty's Air Force assignments forced them to move from base to base. Michelle had fantasized about going to exotic locations overseas. Instead, Marty's tenure was limited to uninspiring outposts in Oklahoma, Alabama and Florida.

Places that would bore Michelle to tears.

"Michelle was getting lonely," Orange said. "Like so many military families, these things take shape early on. Marty would be gone months at a time and of course telephone and e-mail exchanges are not the same as a face to face. Michelle felt entitled to more from life then what she was getting. This isn't uncommon obviously but Michelle took things one step further eventually."

During the occasions when Marty was on leave, he and Michelle would often end up fighting.

"I want children," Marty said.

"No way," Michelle would shake her head, stifling a laugh.

"Then what's the point? What's the point of being married if we are not going to start a family?"

"Raise children in this shithole? You've got to be kidding."

The arguments would escalate. Michelle was a slob, refusing to clean up around the house. Marty would complain but Michelle would deflect and criticize him for his poor career choice.

"You're never home," Michelle hissed. "And you want a family?"

After nine years of marriage, Marty was sent to the Pope Air Force Base near Fayetteville, North Carolina. Fayetteville was considered to be the equivalent of Siberia when it came to transfers. Military members gave the town nicknames like FayetteNam, Fatalville, and FayetteHell. Michelle found the town to be even worse than its reputation when it came to providing excitement.

"Here I was in Fayetteville," Michelle said. "'Loserville'. And I had nobody I could hang out with. Nobody I could pick up a phone and call."

Marty saw things differently, writing on a Christmas card in 2000, "Pope has provided a great change of pace for me and Michelle is happy with her new job. So, 2000 is looking good for both of us."

Michelle would suffer from depression and loneliness after the six years of marriage. Marty tried hard to appease his high-maintenance wife. He took her scuba diving in the Caribbean, skiing in the Rockies, parachuting in Georgia and then a summer marathon run in Alaska.

Despite all of the adventures, Michelle was dissatisfied. She wanted something more out of life, more excitement. She decided to go back to school and earn a degree in psychology. She felt desperately alone, however, as Marty would once again be deployed overseas. Michelle would find work with a psychologist named Dr. Thomas Harbin's and work to obtain her license in psychology.

Still, it wasn't enough. She needed excitement.

More specifically, sexual excitement.

So she turned to the Internet.

Michelle began turning to dating sites. She noodled around with different memberships and it never became more than an idle pursuit to fill the hours of loneliness. Setting up her ad with the headline of "sexy brunette seeks rendezvous man", her inbox was immediately deluged with drooling suitors.

She entertained a number of different men, sending and receiving flirty messages. Michelle had become interested in the local "swinger" and sex club scene, advertising for a man who would be her escort to a club called "Carolina Friends."

One man got her attention more than the others.

JOHN DIAMOND

John was four years younger than Michelle, entering the United States Army during the year in which the couple got married. He had a wandering eye, currently married to his second wife knew of his lothario ways. She was a Panamanian woman who was a few years older than John. He didn't hide his infidelities and on one occasion had one of his girlfriends call the house to ask his wife if John was still meeting her at the beach.

"John loved women," Debbie Dvorak, John's younger sister said. "He loved women, he always had a girlfriend and was a ladies man. My brother was an attractive guy. He had a great personality. His personality made him that much more attractive."

John's background was remarkably similar to Marty in that he was born into a military family. His father was a Vietnam veteran and his grandfather had been a POW during World War II. John himself became an Army ranger and was stationed nearby at Fort Bragg. He was trained as a sniper and highly decorated. Their military backgrounds were where their similarities ended, however. Marty was highly respected as a pilot and a family man. John was a good soldier but nowhere near the honorable family man Marty was.

"John was a highly regarded soldier," Orange said. "But he already had two families. He had a child with his first wife and they divorced. He remarried and had a son with the second wife. So his plate was already full by the time he met Michelle Theer."

John and Michelle both intuitively knew what the other wanted. They both needed the adrenaline, the excitement of forbidden sex to add spice to their humdrum lives. John and Michelle spent months sending each other flirtatious and juicy e-mails before realizing it was time to put fantasy aside and meet for real.

There was an immediate attraction as they met at a Fayetteville coffee shop.

"It was love at first sight," John said.

"I thought he was very, very charming," Michelle said. "He was funny. We talked about movies and music. Things that me and Marty didn't talk about."

They were both still married, however, and that added to the thrill.

LET THE SEDUCTION BEGIN

John and Michelle then began spending as much time with they could with one another. Their extra-marital affair could be done inside Michelle's own bedroom as Marty would be stationed overseas. Michelle grew addicted to the sex, the excitement and the adoration that John gave her.

"He was very attentive," Michelle said. "He was very affectionate. He was very adoring. Yeah, it felt great."

The sex grew addicting for both John and Michelle. Like drug addicts, they found escape through the pleasures of the flesh. E-mails and text messages between the two would reveal a controlling relationship that favored Michelle. He was at her beck and call, like a "puppy dog" said one investigator.

"I can't wait until you come back so we can take care of each other," John wrote in one message. "You know, sex, sex, sex and of course...more sex. I know that we are meant to be together and are kindred soul mates. I will always love you, no matter how you have hurt me."

"I think it was just the sex," Dvorak said when asked what John saw in the married Michelle. "He was obsessed. He was smitten with having sex with her."

Michelle would later reveal to her psychologist that she didn't think that the affair took away from her love for Marty.

"She said that Marty was the love of her life," Orange said. "With John, it was just lust. She never loved him the same way she loved Marty. At least that is how she differentiated and rationalized it in her mind."

Without fear of being caught, the two began going to dance clubs as well as "swinger parties" as a couple at Michelle's request.

"She would take him to these sex clubs," Dvorak said. "She would say 'If you want to go have sex with her, that's okay. That's fine. Go. I'm fine with it.' And he was just like 'Wow, okay.'"

Finding a partner in crime for her sex addiction, Michelle indulged whenever she could.

Then Marty returned home.

REPAIR JOB?

Marty had been undergoing flight maneuvers in Little Rock, Arkansas. When he returned home to Fayetteville, he came back knowing that his marriage was on the rocks. Michelle wanted to go to marriage counseling but Marty refused.

"He wouldn't agree to marriage counseling and I moved out," Michelle said. "He was shocked."

Michelle got her own place that summer. She would spend most of her days and nights in the arms of John Diamond. "He was so attentive," Michelle recalled. "He would rub my feet for five hours if I wanted him to."

John continued to fall deeper in love with Michelle. He thought that she was more intelligent than the women he had dated before, more of a challenge. Three months after living alone, however, Michelle changed her mind about John.

She went back to Marty.

Michelle thought she would give the marriage one more chance. Marty relented on going to counseling and the couple hashed things out with the therapist.

"I want Michelle to clean up around the house more," Marty said to the counselor. "I mean, I know that with women's lib and all that sounds very degrading. But I work my tail off. I'm away for months at a time and would at least like to come home to someplace clean. It shows respect. Coming home to a mess of a house shows a lot of disrespect."

"See what I mean?" Michelle said. "Talk about obsessive-compulsive. Where does a clean house fit in the grand scheme of things? I want to live life. Go out and have new experiences.

But this guy? All he wants to do is stay home. Stay home in his clean house."

The counseling didn't work. In the summer of 2000, Michelle moved out of the family home. She and John found an off-base apartment and began living together. The cheating couple took a vacation to the Netherlands Antilles and fell in love with the place. Michelle enjoyed it so much that she applied to the Saba School of Medicine. She listed John as her next of kin, describing his relationship to her as "fiancee".

But later Michelle would tell her psychologist that her decision to go back with John was a "relapse."

"I knew that I loved Marty," Michelle said. "And I knew that I wanted to make it work. I knew it in my heart."

Then she went back to Marty again.

She continued to see John, however, but the relationship would be on and off. John would plead his case through e-mails, writing flowery messages about how much he loved Michelle.

"I love you so much," John wrote. "I know you feel the same. What I don't understand is how you could be with a man that you don't love anymore. You're unhappy with him. You're happy with me. This is all so confusing."

"He said specifically 'I'm going to kill myself,' Michelle said. "'I can't live without you. You can't do this to me. I'm gonna go drive my car off a bridge.'"

According to Michelle, John would not relent in his pursuit of her. He would show up at her office and make a scene, telling her that he would tell Marty about their affair.

Michelle relented to seeing John one last time, agreeing to meet with John at a local restaurant. According to her statements to her psychologist, she went there in the hopes of ending the affair for good.

"We had that whole talk," Michelle said. "You know, 'we can only be friends' and 'this can never happen again. Never, never, never.' He seemed very calm. Very rational. I told him, 'I don't want to leave my husband.' I never told him, 'I love you.' I never said 'I want to be with you.' I mean, I think I was pretty straight up."

Whether this conversation took place or not, it certainly landed on deaf ears to John. He continued to pursue Michelle and they continued to see one another.

"She probably led him on a roller coaster ride of emotions," military investigator Vincent Bustillo said. "Brought him to the peak, thinking everything was going to be good and they're going to leave this life together, off in some Caribbean island, and then back off and leave Diamond emotionally distraught to the point where that's what he wanted and nothing was going to get in his way."

The on-again, off-again relationship turned red hot by December 9th, 2000. Michelle told Marty that she would be attending a birthday party for a graduate school friend of hers. Thinking nothing of it, Marty simply nodded his head.

Michelle left the home and met John for a night of torrid sex.

"The manipulation began early on in the relationship," Orange said. "Michelle would pull John into her world with sex. Then she would push him away by going back to her husband. John was smitten with her and could not let go. He would have done anything for her and Michelle knew it. An Army ranger willing to do anything for you is a powerful thing. It was like having her own personal soldier willing to kill. But who did she need getting rid of and why?"

Michelle knew that Marty had a half-million dollar insurance policy that he took out in 1999.

She was the sole beneficiary.

John's sister, however, remained adamant that Michelle had written those lovelorn letters to herself in order to put the trail on John Diamond.

"He never once expressed any feelings of love for her to me," Debbie Dvorak said. "Unless you come to me with a handwritten letter that he was obsessed with her, I'll never believe that. He told me he did not want to marry her. He did not want to spend the rest of his life with her. I think she was obsessed with him. Obsessed that she couldn't control him. That she couldn't control the situation."

Eight days later after her latest rendezvous, Michelle would attend a Christmas party given by her employer, Dr. Thomas Harbin. She brought along Marty who seemed to enjoy the company at the otherwise mellow party. About an hour into the get-together, Michelle excused herself to make a phone call.

A phone call to John Diamond.

A short while later, Marty and Michelle drove another couple home before heading to the local gas station.

"We ended up turning around and going back to the office," Michelle said. "To get some stuff that I needed so I could stay up and work that night."

Marty sat in their Ford Explorer and watched as Michelle walked up to the second story office. A few minutes passed and Marty got worried. He got out of the car and went upstairs to her office to make sure his wife was okay.

He reached the top of the stairs and then he was ambushed.

A gunman stepped out from the shadows and fired four times. Marty tumbled down the stairwell. When he reached the bottom, he was still alive.

The shadowy gunman stood above him and fired one more time, killing Marty.

Michelle would state to police that she discovered Marty's body and began screaming his name. She said that she thought he was still breathing but in the haste of living her office she locked her keys inside. Michelle said she ran two miles to a video store to call 911 despite the area having numerous homes and businesses nearby.

Police arrived on scene and found Michelle cradling Marty in her arms, her husband's blood pooling onto the concrete. Military police arrived shortly after the city authorities, getting the case after it was revealed that Marty was an Air Force Captain.

Both police agencies initially suspected that Marty was the victim of a random robbery. They searched the area and found no one despite the fact that Michelle stated that she has "seen someone in the bushes" when she discovered Marty's body.

FIGURING THINGS OUT

Investigators would discover bullet holes at the top of the stairwell as well as sequins from Marty's suit. They surmised that Marty was at the top of the stairwell when he was shot from someone coming from the bottom of the steps. He then fell down the stairs, bleeding but still alive when the attacker delivered the fatal shot to the back of his left ear.

The police then found his wallet with cash and credit cards still on his person. The scene now looked less like a robbery and more like a targeted execution. After recovering the shell casings (a 9mm pistol was the culprit) they went upstairs to Michelle's office. Inside, they discovered that Michelle had used the toilet (and didn't flush) as well as leaving an empty candy wrapper in the trash.

Police noted that it was almost as if she went upstairs to wait *something* out. If she were, in fact, looking for a book, it would not have taken that long.

The police released Michelle on her own recognizance. The next morning, they returned to the office and spoke to her employer, Dr. Harbin. The doctor would reveal that Michelle had been having marital trouble and was having an affair with John Diamond.

Police now saw John Diamond as the man with the motive. But when they interviewed Lourdes Diamond, John's wife, she said that she was home with her husband that entire evening, watching a movie. The police became discouraged.

Then Lourdes added that John got a call about 9 p.m. that evening and that he quickly left the house. She stated that John changed his clothes, put on parka clothing and told her that he had to go to the barracks.

Police then checked out the phone records on John's cell phone and noted that he did receive a call from Michelle.

Michelle would later deny that she ever called John that night.

After receiving the cell phone records, however, it became evident that John and Michelle had called each other twenty times a day at a minimum. They had exchanged a phone call about ninety minutes prior to Marty being shot to death.

When pressed on his involvement with Michelle, John admitted to the affair.

"She is one of many," John said. "She's a side piece. I have a lot of women."

Michelle would later claim that she conducted her own detective work after Marty's death. She stated that she went to John's home and asked him if he knew anything about the murder.

"I asked him 'do you know anything about this," Michelle said. "'Do you know anybody who had anything to do with this?' He said 'No, I would never do anything to hurt you. I know how much you loved him.' I believed him. He looked so trustful."

Police would dismiss Michelle's confrontation with John. They tailed him around town, watching him park in front of the Theer home and sneak inside through the back door.

John would remain there the whole night.

"He knew I was depressed," Michelle said. "And I was getting more and more depressed. I think I went to John for comfort."

John and Michelle would then travel to Florida as Marty's murder investigation was ongoing. The official reason according to Michelle:

Grief counseling.

She claimed there was a former professor there in the state that would be able to help her cope with Marty's death.

While in Florida, John went to live with his sister, Debbie Dvorak.

"He acted as if nothing was wrong," Dvorak said. "He knows he had nothing to do with it. He didn't shoot him."

The physical evidence remained weak. The police continued to sift through the cell phone records and came across the phone number of one of John's army friends. Calling him up, they asked if John would have access to any 9mm weaponry. The friend would reveal that he had, in fact, loaned out his gun to John. The transaction took place just days before Marty's murder. The Smith & Wesson Model 5906 that he loaned John would be the same type of weapon used to kill Marty. All the police had to do was obtain the murder weapon and they would have the physical evidence required to indict.

Then, as if on cue in a mystery movie, John Diamond reported a break-in of his car in the base parking lot.

"Did they steal anything?" a reporting officer asked.

"Yeah," John said. "My friend's gun. Jesus, he's going to be pissed."

But John made a mistake.

There was a pile of glass outside the car which would indicate that the passenger side door had been open during the "break-in". John had smashed the window himself and feared getting glass on the interior of his car.

The US Army investigators would charge John with obstruction of justice, conspiracy, and premeditated murder. The Army officials relayed their findings to civilian police and wanted them to charge Michelle. Five months later, John would be court-martialed. Michelle would be called as a witness but invoke her Fifth Amendment right with every question.

"John would have a cocky air about him throughout his trial," Orange said. "He joked with reporters and smiled at the jury. He felt certain that he would be acquitted."

His cocky demeanor would backfire. The jury would find John guilty and he was convicted of all counts. His current wife Lourdes would testify that John would receive a phone call in the evening and leave the home. His mother-in-law would also testify that he had come home in the middle of the night and began washing clothes.

John would be sentenced to life without parole.

But Michelle Theer remained free.

"What I got from him (John) after he was arrested was that he didn't want anything to do with her," his sister Debbie said. "Nothing. You don't expect to be convicted on theory. On myths. Show me blood. Show me a gun. Show me a time-line that works. Show me those facts. I'll believe until the day I die that she (Michelle) killed her husband, that she planned to have my brother go down for it, so she could live this happy, wonderful life."

"From my opinion, if he (John) wanted to shoot someone he could have shot someone from a mile away. Why sneak up on somebody and shoot them five times and even according to the coroner, they're all over the place. Whoever shot that weapon wasn't a sharp shooter. Didn't know how to shoot a weapon, was scared to be there, whatever, they were all over the place. Ricocheting off of this and ricocheting off of that. There's just no way."

Upon John's conviction, Michelle left town. She moved to New Orleans until the Fayetteville police finally got the grand jury to indict her on charges of first-degree murder in May of 2002.

Michelle fled the city, however, and became a fugitive on the run.

"I think she planned to kill her husband a long time ago," Dvorak said. "I think she waited and researched and waited for that right person who would look and fit the part to pin it on."

During John's trial, Michelle had begun her preparation. She purchased pamphlets such as REBORN IN THE USA, HOW TO DISAPPEAR IN AMERICA, and SECRETS FOR GETTING A NEW IDENTITY, obtaining tips on how to evade detection from authorities. Michelle also obtained a few books on learning Spanish and travel guides to several Latin countries like Mexico. She bleached her hair blonde and used a high-end printer to make both fake birth and baptismal certificates.

Michelle was dead serious about evading capture. Hiding out in Florida, she paid to have plastic surgery done on her nose, chin and had laser surgery to remove her acne and other skin blemishes.

From an appearance standpoint, she had fully reinvented herself. Michelle was able to fool the DMV and get a driver's license under the alias of "Alexandra Solomon." She rented an apartment under the name of "Lisa Pendragon" from Cynthia Geesey in Lauderdale by the Sea, Florida.

"She told me that she was on the run from an abusive boyfriend in California," Geesey said. "I thought she was well-spoken and articulate."

Geesey allowed Michelle to sign the six-month lease, believing her story. Michelle would blend into her surroundings rather easily. She made a few friends around the neighborhood and found a new boyfriend. She then called her parents from a pay phone in town to let them know she was okay.

"She was always a little apprehensive," Geesey said. "Always looking over her shoulder. That's the only thing I found a little strange about her. I was talking to her one day in front of her apartment and there was a helicopter overhead. And she freaked out! Ran back inside. I said 'It's just a helicopter' and she said 'I don't know, it might be my boyfriend.' And I found that a little odd. But other than that she seemed pretty reasonable , paid her rent on time. Took good care of her animals, no other problems with her."

Fayetteville police were at a loss in locating Michelle and enlisted the aid of United States Marshals. True to form, they knew that Michelle could not resist male companionship and caught a break. Michelle instructed her new boyfriend to call her parents from a pay phone in order to relay a message. Her new beau, however, made the mistake of calling Michelle's family from his parent's home. The U.S. Marshals were already tracing all of Michelle's calls and they quickly found out the identity of her new boyfriend.

Placing him under watch, Michelle's new beau soon led authorities straight to her.

After being on the run for three months, Michelle had been finally been captured.

THE AFTERMATH

Michelle's case took two years to go to trial. She would turn down a plea deal which would send her to prison for only ten years. The case then went to trial for ten weeks, drawing both local and national media attention.

Despite the lengthy trial, the jury returned after only six hours of deliberation.

Marty Theer's mother, Linda, waited in nervous anticipation as the verdict was read.

"Guilty."

Linda shook with emotion and tears as the word was spoken. For her, she felt relief that the trial was finally over.

"He (Marty) was a very, very tender person," Linda said. "There wasn't a mean bone in his body. He wouldn't have anything bad to say about anybody. I wish I could say the same."

Michelle would be sentenced to life in prison without the possibility of parole. She is currently housed at the North Carolina Correctional Institute for Women in Raleigh, North Carolina.

John is currently imprisoned at the United States Disciplinary Barracks at Fort Leavenworth, Kansas.

Both John and Michelle have made attempts to obtain a new trial without success.

BETTY LOU WILL KILL YOU

ALICE WILSON

Betty Lou Beets is a perfect historical example of how multifaceted crime can be, how a victim could become an aggressor, or an aggressor may adopt the mask of victimhood, and how all is not necessarily as it seems. Convicted for murdering two men and assaulting or attempting to kill four, Betty Lou's story is one that would send chills down the spine of any man from any era. Only the fourth woman to be executed for murder, despite the overall statistics hovering around forty to fifty cases of capital punishment per year, her crimes were too gruesome and cold for the court to offer her a lesser sentence... or were they? As we shall see when we delve into her history, despite Betty Lou's extensive criminal record and constant charges against her from ex husbands and her own children, the justice system was eager to give her a way out of the death sentence and allow her to live her natural life out in prison. And although there were some mitigating circumstances, it is telling that Betty Lou Beets almost got away with a life sentence in a situation where many others would have been executed without remorse.

Betty Lou Beets was born Betty Lou Dunevant on the 12th of March 1937, in Roxboro, North Carolina, USA. Her parents were initially tobacco farmers, whose main pleasure in life was alcohol, resulting in rampant alcoholism and a violent family life not atypical of the rural poor of the Great Depression. They lived on a diet of salt pork and various flours, barely touching vegetables or fruit, let alone eggs, fish, nuts or pulses, essential for developing a healthy brain and body. Furthermore, Betty Lou was disabled. She was not completely deaf, but hard of hearing due to having contracted the measles some time between the ages of three and six. Her fever was so severe and prolonged that she suffered damage to her brain and ears. As her hearing was affected at such a young age, she suffered an impairment to her speech similar to what many deaf or hard of hearing children suffer. At another time, or in another family, Betty Lou may have received treatment and hearing aids, but as a poor family in 1940, they could not afford to get her the treatment she would have needed to hear and speak normally. Her education was strongly impacted as she could not learn to read or study, resulting in borderline illiteracy and innumeracy and a frustrating life at home and away. Betty Lou also claimed she had been raped by her father in early childhood, as well as sexually abused by others. By the age of twelve her family life was falling apart. Her mother had been institutionalized due to breakdowns caused by alcoholism and Betty Lou had to drop out of school so she could care for her younger brother and sister. Her father, who seemed to see her as a surrogate mother for her siblings, became guarded against any sign of Betty Lou escaping and would beat her for not taking full responsibility for her siblings. She was often at the doctor's office or in hospital for the injuries he inflicted on her. She finally left school completely. The family moved to Hampton, Virginia, while Betty Lou was still a young girl, so that her father could work as a machinist. They were poor, she was young and disabled and she was a victim at the hands of the very people who were supposed to care for her. These circumstances were hardly the healthiest for the young girl to grow up in, and it is not shocking that Betty Lou became increasingly unstable and inclined to criminality in such an environment during such a time of deprivation. However it is also noteworthy that many more people suffered equal or worse hardship, yet did not turn to criminal activity. Perhaps it was the combination of everything, all together at once, but as she grew up something was going very, very wrong inside Betty Lou.

At the age of fifteen she married her first husband, Robert Franklin Branson. Far from an age where anyone feels quite ready to move into adulthood, Betty Lou was married for the first time. She would remain with him for seventeen years before finally divorcing. Although she levied accusations of violence against all her husbands, Robert Franklin

Branson was the only one whose life she did not threaten directly herself. It appears he picked up where her father left off. If she was ever a unilateral victim, this may have been the one time. Within the first year she attempted suicide and became pregnant. They had a daughter together. She also later had a son with Robert Branson, who was also named Robert after his father. They went onto have four more children. Their children may have been a factor in reducing the marital violence, extending the duration of the relationship and, ultimately, saving Robert Branson Senior's life. In 1958 he evicted her from their home and put her on a bus to Virginia while he kept her children, at which point Betty again attempted suicide via an overdose of sleeping pills. They divorced in 1969, which left Betty Lou a financial and emotional wreck.

Being single took its toll on Betty Lou. She attached her self-worth to her ability to stay married. She began drinking to fight her feelings of loneliness. Between her own insecurities and the hard time she had getting money from either Robert Branson or the Welfare service to support her, Betty Lou soon felt she needed to remarry. She married Billy York Lane at the age of thirty two. Their marriage was a tumultuous one, and very short. There was evidence of mutual violence and disregard for each other's wellbeing. Lane had been abusive towards a previous partner and Betty Lou responded to his violence in turn. Her daughters recall how he used to beat her senseless and how she used to attack him. He initially wanted to charge her for attempted murder, but swiftly dropped the charges after he was forced to admit he had attacked her, broken her nose and threatened her life. They divorced the same year and remarried again shortly after the trial. After Betty Lou shot at him, Billy York Lane divorced her again, only a month after their remarriage, this time for good. It would prove the wisest decision of his life, as her subsequent husbands found out.

Betty Lou remained single for a year and unmarried for eight more years. During the interim Betty Lou worked in a warehouse, then took up work at a topless bar to cover the bills. She sent two of their children back home to Branson, as she could not afford to care for them. She went on to marry Ronnie C. Threlkold, her boyfriend of seven years, at the age of forty. However this relationship would be as unpredictable, violent and dangerous for Ronnie as it was for Billy. In this case there was little evidence Ronnie had been violent towards Betty Lou, although she accused him of violence at later dates, but her habits had been firmly cemented and she continued to display abusive behaviour towards him. She also continued to work at the topless bar, resulting in arrests and thirty days in country jail under the charge of public lewdness. Despite their seven year courtship, the marriage lasted just a year, culminating in Betty Lou Beets's attempted homicide of Ronnie in 1978, where she shot him in the stomach, wounding him, and their divorce in 1979.

She married Doyle Wayne Barker at the age of forty one, closely after her divorce from Threlkold. Their marriage lasted a mere seven weeks before her violent behaviour drove Doyle away from her. However his own violence was undeniable. He had stalked her, assaulted her and raped her during their short relationship. The day he left Betty Lou had bruises all over her face, neck, arms and chest. There is no available record of the divorce, however all living parties assumed it had taken place. However Doyle Wayne did not get out of their marriage unscathed. He disappeared after their divorce and his body was found years later, buried under a garage, killed by three gunshots.

But this grisly deed was not uncovered for many more years to come. Rather, Betty Lou went on to marry a firefighter named Jimmy Don Beets, her final husband, at the age of forty four.

"Jimmy Don Beets was a wonderful man," said a family friend. "He was loved by so many people. An old country boy that a lot people had respect for."

Their courtship would last a mere six months. Betty Lou would meet Jimmy while she worked as a waitress and the seduction began. Her two sons moved in with them. This would be her final marriage, and her actions within it would be her undoing. Although their courtship had been pleasant, they both suffered from alcoholism, which slowly drove their marriage to the same violence she had experienced previously. Less than a year later she murdered him by gunshot, and this time she was caught. Robert Branson, her son from her first marriage, had been informed that she intended to kill her last husband, telling him to steer clear of the residence as the murder took place. On the 6th of August 1983, Robert Branson Junior left their home and Betty Lou Beets committed the gruesome act. Not only did Robert provide evidence that the act was premeditated, but he also was expected to participate. Two hours after leaving the house, Robert Branson Junior returned, finding his step father dead with two gunshot wounds in his body. Rather than seek assistance, Robert Branson Junior, either tainted by a lifetime with a mother who viewed abuse and murder as daily events or himself an individual with low empathy, helped his mother to dispose of the body. Betty Lou Beets and Robert Branson Junior carted Jimmy Don Beets' body outside to an ornamental wishing well that stood in the front yard of their house. Undetected, they cast the body inside.

Then, Betty Lou returned to the house to cover up her acts. She called the police to report her husband missing from their Cedar Creek Lake home. The next day, Betty Lou became more devious. Perhaps inspired, perhaps unnerved by her success killing Doyle Wayne Barker, she realized she needed to create a story with which to divert the police from her trail. Robert Branson Junior recalled to the press how she had taken some of Jimmy Don Beets's heart medication down to his boat at the lake. Then she had removed the propeller, placed the medication in the boat and abandoned it, floating loosely in the water. Later that day, as the twenty four hours since Jimmy Don Beets's initial disappearance drew to a close, various officials began the search for the presumably missing man. Officers from the Henderson County Sheriff's department, various members of the fire department, as well as agents from the Texas Parks and Wildlife department searched for three weeks. They naturally found no body. However they did find Jimmy Don Beets's boat drifting in the lake, near to the Redwood Beach Marina. There they found his fishing license, an unused life jacket and the heart medication which Betty Lou Beets had placed there. Not knowing anything about the murder or the forged evidence, they brought Betty Lou Beets to the Marina as the sole witness, where she identified the boat and its contents as those of her husband. Although no body had been recovered, it was considered case closed.

Betty Lou Beets would have likely got away with both murders, were it not for confidential information given to the Henderson County Sheriff's Department two years later. The information suggested that Jimmy Don Beets had not disappeared innocently, and that his assumed death, with no body that had been found, may be the result of foul play. The evidence was enough that the cold case was reopened in Spring 1985. As their suspicions became stronger, the investigators were drawn to Betty Lou Beets, who was arrested on the 8th of June of 1985 and then booked into the Henderson County Jail. An officer on the case, Rick Rose, who had been in charge of her arrest warrant, secured a further warrant to search the Beets's home and lands, including the yard. Ultimately, they discovered Jimmy Don Beets's remains buried under the wishing well where he had been left two years prior. But another discovery would surface that would further disturb the case. Also in the back yard was a storage shed which could be moved. When the officers moved it, something compelled them to disturb the soil that had lain there several years. Perhaps it was some confidential evidence or perhaps it was just intuition, but it paid off when they discovered a second body. Doyle Wayne Barker, still missing, was buried there, with three bullets in his body. All five bullets matched the .38 caliber pistol which had been seized from their home after another incident of Betty Lou's violent outbursts. Thanks to the calls she had made the very day of his disappearance there was no room to argue that she had been abusing drugs or alcohol at the time, but there had been no physical evidence that suggested to detectives at the time that Jimmy Don had been abusing her when the incident took place. Her position was weak.

Faced with the evidence, Robert Branson Junior and his sister Shirley finally confessed to their awareness of the killings, as well as their hand in the crimes that had taken place. Not only had Betty Lou told her son about the murder, but she had also informed her daughter, by the Shirley Stegner and not living at the family home, that she planned on killing her husband. Shirley was motivated by her confession to also confess to her involvement in another crime. She told the detectives that she had been involved in the burial of Doyle Wayne Barker's body in October of 1981 after Betty Lou had shot him to death.

In an effort to make herself more likeable to the jury, Betty Lou Beets raised her history of domestic violence as an excuse for her violent behaviour, levying charges against all her prior husbands, as well as her father. However, this would be the first that anyone had heard of most of these charges. This may have been due to attitudes of the times, a desire to protect her children, or the apparently two-sided nature of most of these incidents, however the jury would not believe her claims. They were just too convenient. Instead, it was clear to them that Betty Lou Beets was an unstable and dangerous woman and the only connection between the five men she married and their violence. Whatever the situation was, her psychological well being was never considered during the trial. Despite the obvious impact her upbringing and life would have on her mental state and the fact that her actions up until that point were indicative of definite mental illness, the trial system of the time did not account for that.

Furthermore, the premeditated nature of her actions was evident through her children's abundant testimonials, where they confessed she had shared her intent to kill not only the husbands she managed to murder, but that she had expressed a desire to kill all the men she had been married to. Not only that, but her success concealing the bodies, under the wishing well and under the garden shed, showed a lack of remorse and serious consideration of her crimes. However it seems Betty Lou had not been as careful as she thought. As soon as the trial began, various other witnesses emerged to testify against her. Various people recalled her attempting to collect life insurance of over a hundred thousand dollars as well as a pension of over a thousand dollars a month after Jimmy Don's declared death. A year after the official death of Jimmy Don Beets, she successfully sold his boat, the primary evidence that he had disappeared. She claimed she did not know about his pension or insurance, however seeing as Jimmy Don Beets was already retired and claiming his pension, this claim fell short. Furthermore, had she no awareness of them she would not have pursued either so actively. She claimed she had been told about them when she visited an attorney by the name or E. Ray Andrews about a fire insurance claim she needed to make, at which point he discovered she could claim his insurance and pension. However her own filing for these benefits did not align with the supposed visit, and the only person who could say for sure that she had not known about her deceased husband's finances was E. Ray Andrews himself, who agreed to represent her in exchange for the rights to book and movie deals concerning her life and case.

Betty Lou Beets was indicted for murder for remuneration or the promise of remuneration, with her recovery of his life insurance and pension as evidence. She plead not guilty and was taken to trial, where she was found guilty of the capital offence of first degree murder on the 11th of October of 1985. She was found again guilty during a hearing on the 14th of October 1985 and was sentenced to death by the trial court. This was due to her prior history of violence and attempted murders, which suggested that she would present a threat to others in the future, specifically to any man who entered a relationship with her again. Yet her conviction and sentence were quickly and successfully appealed to the Texas Court of Criminal Appeals. Such was the situation that, under Texas law, crime for the sake of insurance and pension claims was not covered by the definition of "murder for remuneration", instead falling into two separate categories of first degree murder and insurance fraud, or crime with intent to commit insurance fraud. The Texas Court of Criminal Appeals reversed her conviction for capital murder, citing the Texas Penal Code as evidence that her particular case could not be filed as "murder for remuneration".

The State then requested a rehearing of the cause. Although her original conviction had been overturned, the fact remained that Betty Lou Beets was guilty of homicide under some circumstance or another.

On the 21st of September of 1988, the Court of Criminal Appeals reinstated her conviction and sentence based on the evidence received. Betty Lou Beets was on death row. Her execution was scheduled for the 8th of November 1989.

However her court case did not go as it should have in the first place. Attorney E. Ray Andrews was heavily invested in sensationalizing her case as much as he could, seeing as he would profit enormously from the case blowing up into a media phenomenon. So although she claimed and he later agreed that she had known nothing of her husband's finances, the trial was conducted under the assumption that she was fully aware of the money she would receive. Not only that, but E. Ray Andrews did everything in his power to create a more dramatic case on both sides, which ultimately meant excluding Betty Lou from much of the information about her own trial. Betty Lou was becoming desperate at this point. Although she had a long history of domestic violence, attempted murder and two bodies in her garden, she decided to attempt to blame the murder of Jimmy Don Beets on Robert Branson Junior, her own son. She did not seem to have made the statement in sound mind, but E. Ray Andrews allowed her to speak on her own behalf and did not retract it, as it added dramatic quality to the event. He tried to cover up later, saying that Betty Lou had possibly been taking the blame for her son, however he had no proof other than that Robert Branson Junior was male and from a rough background. This statement and its acceptance horrified the court, as it was alarming to them to see a mother who, rather than protect her children, was willing to throw them under the bus by falsely accusing them of a crime she had more than evidently committed. Furthermore, by admitting and adhering to the story that Robert Branson Junior was in fact the actual killer, Betty Lou lost all chances of arguing that she acted in self-defence and made her own accusations of domestic violence against Jimmy Don and her prior husbands completely irrelevant. This is despite the fact that a leading domestic violence specialist of the time believed Betty Lou Beets had been significantly mentally impacted by her experiences, and that she suffered "the emotional, cognitive, and behavioural components of battered woman syndrome, rape trauma syndrome, and PTSD" which he added must have interacted with her pre-existing organic brain damage from her childhood illness, history of battering and substance abuse. All together, this would have presented a robust case for her mental illness and need for treatment rather than punishment. However E. Ray Andrews discarded this option in favour of the more dramatic choice of supporting Betty Lou's accusation against her son. They became stuck in the position of having to argue she did not kill her husband at all. This context may have reduced her sentence, or made her eligible to claim insanity. However neither of these options were available.

Throughout the entire case, E. Ray Andrews failed to represent her seriously and did nothing to prevent her from shooting herself in the foot repeatedly. In fact, seeing the case was a lost cause and that he stood to gain more from her sentence than her freedom, Andrews began drinking heavily for the duration of the trial. He chose not to bear witness to her claims that she did not know about Jimmy Don Beets's pension or insurance, which would have transformed the case to one of murder in the context of domestic violence, rather than murder for remuneration. He managed to offer the jury no reasons to consider that Betty Lou was not a serious threat to those around her, eventually sealing her fate. Yet he remained her attorney for the duration of her appeal as well. It was he who raised the point that her financial gain was not necessarily the motivator for murder, but a by product. He also finally raised that she was not aware of the insurance or pension until she spoke to him, however this was met with scepticism due to his negligence to mention it any sooner, and was perceived as a lie in effort to overturn Betty Lou's criminal charges after his initial failure to protect her.

On the 16th of October 1989, Betty Lou filed a motion called a stay of execution which would delay her execution to give her time to prepare and file a habeas corpus application with the state. On the 1st of November she filed the application and the trial court delayed her execution so that the claims she was raising, such as consideration towards her mental state and marital conditions, could be properly addressed. During this time Betty Lou wrote several letters from prison in which she attempted to defend her good name and that of her last husband. She attempted to balance the accusations that she was a black widow by reminding the court that she was Jimmy Don's fourth wife as well. However his previous wives did not come forward to support her. She also defended her own identity, denying that she ever worked as a barmaid, regardless of her own charges for lewd behaviour, and that she was never on welfare, despite her claims after her first divorce. She also said that the Fire Department Chaplain, who stated he had informed her about Beets's insurance and pension, had spoken to her sister in law, Betty Beets, instead. She even quibbled over the descriptions of her garden, insisting the well was a planter in the shape of a well and not an actual well. It was clear that Betty Lou Beets was desperate to save face and project a more pleasant, more ordinary identity than the one which E. Ray Andrews had created for her in the courtroom. It was also clear that her mental health was degrading as she endured life in prison and submitted her habeas corpus petition. In her petition she argued against her sentence of the death penalty, raising issues such as the alleged value Jimmy Don Beets apparently added the community, the testimonials of victims and sufferers whose statements were unconstitutional under the Victim Impact Statements act of 1987, and the poor assistance which E. Ray Andrews provided, especially regarding her history of domestic abuse. Yet without his help in writing and presenting the letter, her claims were weak and not fully backed by legal evidence. Andrews did not visit her from the point of her sentencing and prepared for her trials without ever speaking to her. Furthermore, she could have claimed that his services were provided against American Bar Association rules, which prohibit the trade of legal services for copyright issues, such as the rights to her case. None of this was raised by her against him, and as such it was not considered during her habeas corpus appeal.

However on the 27th of June her appeal for state habeas corpus was turned away. She was placed in the position of proving that, had E. Ray Andrews presented a testimony about her lack of awareness of the insurance and her history of domestic violence, the jury would have judged her not guilty of a capital crime. Without a proper attorney to defend her, it would be impossible for Betty Lou to prove this was the case, and the court deemed Andrews's mistakes to have been harmless to her trial. The Fifth Circuit Court of Appeals went on to turn down her final appeals. The judges remained convinced that, regardless of any remaining evidence, Betty Lou Beets's history of violence and attempted murder, along with the two concealed bodies in her garden, were evidence enough that a death sentence was a fair response to the crime that had taken place. She had displayed violence her whole life, even towards men who had not presented a threat to her, and had attempted to kill all but one of her husbands. She had concealed her murders carefully and for many years and was willing to place the blame on her own adult son. In other words, regardless of her own situation, her criminal intent was viewed as evident and incorrigible, and her death sentence was the only fitting end to her crime spree.

On death row, Betty Lou Beets retained some supporters, mostly her own children. Some of Betty Lou's daughters went to E. Ray Andrews with photographic evidence of the domestic abuse she had suffered in order to request a parole review, but were declined. They insisted on presenting the evidence that she had suffered and that her acts of violence were a result of brain damage and abuse, not of malicious intent. Faye Lane, one of her daughters, insisted that her mother would only have done anything so horrific if she believed she was abused. Domestic violence awareness groups and charities acting against the death sentence appealed to have her sentence changed to a life sentence in prison, based not only on her own suffering, but on their universal stance against the irreversible process of the death penalty. Yet even those defending her maintained that she was a violent, unpredictable woman and not safe to exit into the general public.

And not all her children were so kind. Shirley told the press that Doyle Wayne Barker was killed because he owned the trailer where they lived, and that after the divorce which Barker had initiated, Betty Lou and her children would be evicted from the trailer and left homeless. This set a precedent where even her own daughter could not believe that Betty Lou was completely unaware of the financial benefits of murdering Jimmy Don Beets, especially not after she had successfully killed Barker. Knowing that she was still doubted and seeing hope as ever distant, Betty Lou composed her memoirs from death row, presenting her case.

Beets turned to her last resort which was to appeal to then-governor George W. Bush to spare her life. After a media incident where he jokingly insulted the last woman to be executed in Texas in an insensitive manner, George W. Bush seemed keen to prove he had no bias against women, even in the prison system, and agreed to review her case. This would have meant hearing the witnesses which had not been heard by the trial lawyer and present a case against her execution based on the circumstances of her life, including medical and psychiatric evidence. He could have granted her a thirty day reprieve in which he made his decision, however this never materialized. His number was made available and he received thousands of calls and letters from people urging him to spare her, with only fifty seven endorsing her sentence. Yet he did not grant the reprieve or halt the execution.

Betty Lou Beets was finally executed on the 24th of February of 2000, via lethal injection. Protestors from various organisations gathered outside as her sentence awaited. She declined both her last meal and her final statement, having been given by then enough time to make sense of what was happening and to say everything which needed to be said. Strapped to the death chamber gurney, she received her injection at six pm and died within eighteen minutes. She was sixty two years old. She left behind five adult children, nine grandchildren and six great-grandchildren, as well as her memoirs. Her story may be shocking, and it may be hard to pick sides at times, but that is exactly why her trial presents a solid case against the black and white ideals the court system held regarding crime and punishment, perpetrator and victim, defence and offence. Someone can at once be a victim of horrific crimes and a perpetrator of them, at once be a defendant and raise accusations, at once deserve punishment yet suffer a crime gone unpunished. There is no doubt that Betty Lou Beets was a violent woman who invited violence into her own life, an alcoholic and a murderer. However there is no doubt either that she was a good mother within her capacity, a victim of a series of horrific crimes, a disabled person with a background she could not escape and a desperate woman who saw no way out of her situation. Neither black nor white, good not bad, Betty Lou Beets sits in the grey areas of the law.

KILLER CRYSTAL MAE WAGNER

ANA BENSON

History shows us that men are most likely to commit heinous crimes but women are no strangers to violence either. Yes, they do not kill frequently and female killers do not engage in killing sprees so often. Instead, their crimes are driven by passion and sometimes even obsession with another person. They are not prone to selecting a random victim but would turn on their partners, friends, or family. Women are usually not killing for the thrill but they do so for their own personal gain, even if it seems illogical to a bystander. So as you may already know, whenever a body turns up somewhere, the police would immediately question the closest family members.

Crystal Mae Wagner's case is intriguing because she managed to include a third man into the whole narrative and make him do the dirty job for her. The overly brutal killing and the disposal of the body shocked the Bibb County in Georgia. Luckily, Crystal Mae Wagner's body count didn't escalate and she was caught in time. But the trial and the analysis of her psychological profile intrigued everyone who was involved in this case. What makes a loving mother turn on her husband? And was there something that pushed her over the edge to seek help from her lover in order to do this gruesome murder? Let's dive in deeper into this case and discover more details about Crystal Mae Wagner and her life.

Early life

Crystal Mae Wagner (née Carver) was born in 1980 and grew up with her grandparents, mother, and an uncle. The Carvers were a tight family that kept to themselves but remained close to their relatives who were living in the same area. The identity of Crystal Mae's father was unknown. However, a rumor that her uncle is her actual father kept circulating among the neighbors. Crystal Mae was diagnosed with rheumatoid arthritis at a very young age and this horrible illness will leave a permanent mark on her physique. This is an autoimmune disease that makes your own body turn on itself and destroy the tissue. She was left with physical deformities on her joints and skin.

Crystal Mae's childhood wasn't easy at all. Besides rheumatoid arthritis that caused great pain to her body, she was also physically and mentally abused by her family members. She would often be ignored and left to take care of herself without any help from those who were closest to her. The feeling of loneliness would be predominant in her early life and she desperately needed someone who would make her feel wanted. She felt like her family didn't need her at all and that she was unwelcome in her own home. On the other hand, she was often locked in the house and was forbidden from going out. Crystal Mae had no friends which undoubtedly took a toll on her mental state. Her views on emotional relationships were influenced by the lack of affection she got from her mother and grandparents. Crystal Mae was certain that the only way to attract someone is to act like "a piece of meat" and do anything that was asked of her even if she didn't feel like it.

So when Crystal Mae met her future husband, she saw him as the way out of the abusive and loveless environment she grew up in. It didn't matter that Bobby Gene Wagner was seven years older than her. Crystal Mae loved the attention she was getting from him and felt like she finally belonged somewhere. Bobby Gene Wagner had a steady job and he was capable of supporting Crystal Mae. The pair got married soon after and they had a son. But things got a bit rocky after some time. Crystal Mae and Bobby Gene decided to take some time off and see other people. She was only twenty-two years old and wanted to explore different things after gaining her independence.

Crystal Mae Wagner met Shay Alan Morey while she was estranged from her husband. They were the same age and clicked almost immediately. Their romance blossomed quickly and he accepted Crystal Mae's son as his own. However, Crystal Mae Wagner got back together with her husband and the family was back together. She continued to see Shay Alan Morey every now and then. It seems like Bobby Gene Wagner was oblivious to his wife's affair even though he met Shay Alan Morey and the two of them would end up spending a lot of time together.

The couple moved into a south Macon motel called Travel Inn which is located near the Interstate 475. Their son lived with them as well. Shay Alan Morey would join them in the motel but he was in a separate room. Bobby Gene Wagner was certain that Morey was still just a friend and that he was helping Crystal Mae with the toddler. Bobby Gene worked at Heart of Georgia Towing Company and he was really well liked there. He was an excellent employee that never complained and truly enjoyed his job. Bobby Gene Wagner loved both Crystal Mae and their little boy so he was very happy to provide them with everything they needed. He even tried to find Shay Alan Morey a position at the firm and help him get his life back on track.

Unfortunately, the situation between the three of them would turn sour pretty quickly and Bobby Gene Wagner would end up dead. There were no signs that could have warned Bobby Gene on what was about to unfold in their motel room.

The murder

Crystal Mae Wagner and Shay Alan Morey talked about the murder at least a couple of days prior to the crime itself. They discussed everything in detail and made a quick plan that involved the exact manner of the killing and the body disposal site. What prompted Crystal Mae Wagner to start thinking about eliminating her husband is still unclear but her relatives would later say that she felt like she had no freedom in the marriage and that the fact that she was tied down to one man was suffocating her. So she confided in her lover who was willing to do the dirty work for her in order to prove his devotion and love. Crystal Mae didn't even consider getting a divorce and though that the only way she could be with Shay Alan Morey was to completely erase Bobby Gene from her life.

The plan was to get Bobby Gene Wagner into the motel room's bathroom with the story that the entire family is invited to a birthday party and that he needed to get ready as soon as possible. Shay Alan Morey would enter the bathroom and murder Bobby Gene quickly and without making a huge mess. Crystal Mae was certain that the best way to hide Bobby Gene's corpse is to tie him down to a heavy object and submerge him in the water. The police would later discover cinder blocks and cables stashed in both the motel room and Crystal Mae's vehicle.

But even the best plans do fail somewhere along the way and this happened in the murder of Bobby Gene Wagner as well. It was February the 10th 2005 when Bobby Gene Wagner entered the bathroom. His wife told him to get cleaned up because they will be visiting some family friends. Shay Alan Morey waited outside and as soon as Crystal Mae gave him the signal, he burst into the bathroom and started beating Bobby Gene who was in the shower. He was clearly startled and didn't fight back. Even though Shay Alan Morey injured him badly, Bobby Gene was still alive and conscious. He was bleeding and had visible bruises all over his body but that didn't prevent him from going back to his room and telling Crystal Mae what happened. He asked her to call the ambulance and the police because he was attacked. Crystal Mae ignored him and the couple went back to the bathroom together. She left the bathroom and went straight to Shay Alan Morey's room to inform him that her husband is calling the police.

Shay Alan Morey quickly returned to the scene of the crime and launched himself on Bobby Gene. He stabbed him straight into the heart, delivering the fatal blow that left Bobby Gene dead on the spot. The lovers started to panic because it was obvious that it would be very difficult to carry out Bobby Gene's corpse from the motel without being seen. Plus, Bobby Gene was a large man and Shay Alan Morey was simply not strong enough to do it on his own. Therefore, his only option was to dismember Bobby Gene's body and load him up in the car once piece at the time. It is also important to mention that Crystal

Mae's and Bobby Gene's two-year-old son was present in the room while all of this was happening, including the murder of his father.

The plans to go to a river or a lake with the cinder blocks fell through and Shay Alan Morey decided to leave the body behind an abandoned house that was rarely visited by anyone living in the area. He tried to conceal Bobby Gene Wagner's identity by burning his face but left plenty of clues on the spot. Morey didn't stop there but tried to pile up various garbage and aluminum construction pieces on top of the corpse. However, his behavior on the disposal site was unorganized and even left the tools he used back in the motel in order to cut up Bobby Gene's lifeless body.

The discovery of the body

Even though the location that was chosen by Shay Alan Morey was remote and pretty secluded, it took only four days for Bobby Gene's body to be discovered. The first clue that something was wrong was the fact that Bobby Gene Wagner failed to show up at his workplace on the day after the murder. His boss, Robert Allen Wagner called him several times but got no answer. He knew that Bobby Gene sometimes talked about his rocky marriage so he drove to the motel in order to see if everything was alright. Robert Allen Wagner noticed that Bobby Gene's car was parked in the parking lot in front of the motel so he expected to find him in his room. He knocked on the door for a couple of minutes but nobody answered.

Robert Allen Wagner gave up and decided to return the next day. The second try was successful and he was greeted by Shay Alan Morey. Crystal Mae and her son stood behind him in the doorway. They told Robert that Bobby Gene suddenly decided to go to Florida. Robert could see that the motel room was chaotic and that the clothes and trash were all over the place. He would later tell the law enforcement: "That room was a total mess. The odor was so bad I could hardly go in." In the meantime, the authorities discovered Bobby Gene Wagner's body in Twiggs County. The scene was horrifying because the body was dismembered and burned by fire. They managed to find Bobby Gene's wallet that had his ID card inside and a letter with his current place of residence. They discovered his cellphone nearby as well. They checked the call list for his number and saw that he tried to contact the sheriff's office on the 10th of February.

Due to the nature of this crime, the detectives were certain that someone who was close to Bobby Gene Wagner was the perpetrator. They immediately drove to the motel and found the room he was staying in with his wife and child. Crystal Mae Wagner was in there and she appeared to be shocked when the investigators told her that they have discovered her husband's remains. She repeated the Florida story but when the detectives presented her with their own timeline that included the exact date of the call to the sheriff's office, she made a claim that she was sleeping in their motel room while the crime was being committed. Crystal Mae Wagner also mentioned that she drank "a sleeping potion" that knocked her out completely and she couldn't register what was going on around her. Her second statement did not include the so-called sleeping potion so it was obvious to the detectives that Crystal Mae was lying.

Crystal Mae Wagner and Shay Alan Morey were arrested while they were attempting to pick up Bobby Gene Wagner's last paycheck. The scene itself was quite traumatic because both of them were crying and were visibly upset. Department of Family and Children Services picked up Crystal Mae's two-year-old boy. Crystal Mae Wagner's story was filled with holes and she finally pointed her finger in the right direction. She told the detectives who were working on the case that Shay Alan Morey was the killer. However, she also added that Morey was threatening to murder her and her son if she turned him to the authorities. That was the way to justify the fact that she lied to the detectives in her previous statements. She was arrested five days after the murder and Bibb County was getting ready for the trial of both Crystal Mae Wagner and Shay Alan Morey.

The investigation and Morey's trial

The authorities immediately knew the identity of their victim but they needed to get a couple of things straight regarding the crime scene. Since they had both Shay Alan Morey and Crystal Mae Wagner in the custody, they headed straight to the motel room at the Travel Inn. After thorough testing, they concluded that the murder took place in the bathroom and the bathtub was used in order to drain the blood and reduce the possible mess during the dismemberment of the murder victim. The crime itself was starting to look grislier than they thought at first.

Crystal Mae Wagner stopped denying her knowledge about the crime but she stood by the claim that her life and the life of her baby boy were in danger if she told the authorities what happened. She even said to the detectives that she was present when Shay Alan Morey was purchasing the tools he would later on use for cutting up Bobby Gene Wagner's body. She sat in the car while Shay Alan loaded up a hatchet and a mallet into the trunk. She told the investigators that he choose Twiggs County as the location for body disposal because it is quite rural but the detectives were a bit skeptical about this claim. Crystal Mae's grandmother lived close by so the spot was probably chosen because she knew about it prior to the murder and could provide Shay Alan Morey with the directions on how to get there.

The police investigators started digging deeper into the lives of both the victim and the perpetrators. A large number of witnesses that included friends and relatives of both Crystal Mae and Bobby Gene talked to the authorities and filled up the holes in the story that painted a picture of an abusive marriage.

After speaking to Bobby Gene's friends and family, they discovered that the marriage between him and Crystal Mae was troubled from the very beginning. Bobby Gene Wagner had a tendency to fall for difficult women and all of his previous relationships were off and on. So when the two of them met, the pattern was repeated. Bobby Gene was an alcoholic and was very loud when he was drunk, but his friends and family loved him for his eagerness to help and be there for everyone when he was clean and sober. The couple got married when Crystal Mae was twenty-one years old back in 2001 and they soon got a baby boy who became the focus of Bobby Gene's attention. He was a hard worker before but he took extra hours in order to provide his son with everything he might need. However, his boss at Heart of Georgia Towing Company did notice that Bobby Gene Wagner was reluctant to go home after work and would often stay at the headquarters. When his boss tried talking to him about it, Bobby Gene told him that Crystal Mae was behaving erratically and that he was afraid for his life. He even mentioned to one friend that Crystal Mae tried to poison him on one occasion. Bobby Gene filed for a divorce one year after the birth of their baby.

Crystal Mae Wagner met Shay Alan Morey during that time and the two started a relationship. Bobby Gene Wagner wanted to get back together with his estranged wife for the sake of their child so he made a decision to forget and forgive everything that Crystal Mae put him through in the past. His only goal was to try and provide the best possible future for his baby boy. On the other hand, Crystal Mae wasn't ready to let go of her lover and he stayed in the picture. The investigators weren't able to pinpoint the motive for this murder at first and they were as confused as everyone else. But Shay Alan Morey started talking soon after the arrest and confessed that Crystal Mae told him that the only way they could be together was to eliminate Bobby Gene from their lives. He also told them that Crystal Mae was the perpetrator and that she attacked her husband in the bathroom. The story itself got even more confusing at this point because the detectives knew that they had the right people in the custody but the events were still unclear.

The investigators who were talking to Crystal Mae Wagner immediately noticed that her hands were very deformed. She told them about her illness and that she suffered from rheumatoid arthritis. Her hands were simply not strong enough for her to deliver the fatal blow to her husband or use a hatchet in order to dismember a body in a bathtub. As a matter of fact, her fingers and joints were disfigured. Therefore, the detectives knew that the only person who could have physically attack Bobby Gene Wagner was Shay Alan Morey. The case itself was becoming very solid and the investigators were certain that they had a good case against the lovers.

Shay Alan Morey was put to trial first. After all, he was the one who attacked and murdered Bobby Gene Wagner. Since the detectives managed to collect numerous evidence, including the murder weapon, the hearings didn't last a long time. Shay Alan Morey continued to claim that Crystal Mae Wagner was behind the murder and that she knew exactly what he was doing. As a matter of fact, Crystal Mae was pulling all the strings while he was simply "the muscle". He didn't deny that he was involved. Shay Alan Morey pleaded guilty to the murder of Bobby Gene Wagner in March of 2006, just thirteen months after the crime. He received a life sentence without the possibility of the parole. Morey was visibly upset when the judge delivered the sentence and his emotions got the best of him. He wept and cried as he was led out of the courtroom. Bibb County police force started gathering up the evidence for the second trial because it was time to prosecute Crystal Mae Wagner who was, after all, the one who came up with the plan to murder her husband.

The trial of Crystal Mae

Crystal Mae Wagner was expected to receive a death penalty but she gave up her right to a trial in front of a jury. It was a smart move by her defense team because they knew that she would have been found guilty. Instead, all witnesses were called to talk in front of a judge. Crystal Mae's team consisted of Frank Hogue and Laura D. Hogue. Their case relied heavily on the fact that Crystal Mae was abused as a child. After a psychological evaluation, a doctor discovered that she did have the abandonment issues and that Crystal needed someone to be with her at all times. She loved the attention and the fact that two men were fighting for her affections did bring out the worst out of her.

Bobby Gene Wagner's friends told a different story. Even though Crystal Mae had physical disabilities, she was very abusive towards her husband. The prosecution unsealed the divorce documents from 2004 and discovered a number of disturbing details that painted a different picture of Crystal Mae. Bobby Gene told his divorce attorneys that Crystal Mae was a violent drug abuser. Crystal Mae fired back and accused Bobby Gene of trying to choke her. Since Bobby Gene was physically stronger than Crystal Mae, her story sounded more believable. James Davis who was Bobby Gene Wagner's attorney during the divorce hearings told the judge that Bobby Gene confessed to him off the records that Crystal Mae would start the violence by attacking him first and he simply couldn't let her assault him without fighting back. Bobby Gene would later admit to the domestic violence and he was put on a probation in 2004. The couple got back together that same year and Crystal Mae retracted her story.

A couple of Bobby Gene's friends took the stand and told the judge about the relationship between the accused and the victim. Howard Schurter knew Bobby Gene for years and he even moved into Bobby Gene's old trailer which he shared with Crystal Mae at one time. He told the court that Bobby Gene would often leave things in the trailer because he wanted to keep them hidden from Crystal Mae. A lot of his personal documents and the divorce papers were left in Schurter's trailer. Jason Tanner used to live with Bobby Gene Wagner and knew the man pretty well. He described him as someone who had a big heart but would always end up with a wrong kind of women. Bobby Gene Wagner had a failed marriage in the past. He was involved with a woman called Michelle from Kentucky back in the 1990s. He really hoped that his second marriage would be different. Jason Tanner also added: "He was just trying to find somebody to love him. And he wanted to take care of his kid. That man worked 16 hours a day."

Escaping an abusive partner is very difficult regardless of a gender and William Smith who used to work with Bobby Gene Wagner at Precision Tune confirmed that Bobby Gene was in fear for his own life even years before the murder occurred. He told the judge that Bobby Gene would sometimes complain to his co-workers that his wife is going to kill him but would act like nothing was wrong only a couple of days later. When Crystal Mae's relatives took the stand, they were on her side, confirming the story of the abuse and neglect that she suffered in her youth. Marsha Mathews who is closely related to Crystal Mae Wagner did not support her innocence but was listed as her witness. She did her best to shed some light on the motive itself even though she didn't get a chance to speak in front of a judge. She said the following to the reporters: "I feel she felt trapped over the years." It seemed like Crystal Mae Wagner wanted to get out of her marriage with Bobby Gene Wagner and instead of filing for a divorce, she decided to involve her lover. The lead prosecutor Elizabeth Bobbitt also presented a crucial piece of evidence – a letter written by Crystal Mae to Shay Alan Morey in which she discusses the details of the murder.

Crystal Mae Wagner pleaded guilty to murder on 17th of March 2010, ending a long trial process. Just like Shay Alan Morey, she was sentenced to life in prison. Crystal Mae Wagner was tearful during the entire course of the sentencing and broke down when the judge delivered the verdict. She is serving her sentence at the moment and will not be eligible for a parole. Bobby Gene's and Crystal Mae's son was taken in by his maternal grandmother.

KILLER TEEN NIKKI REYNOLDS

SAMANTHA REED

It is not often that stories appear where we find the perpetrators of violence being children and the victims being parents. Although, scattered throughout history it has been seen that children can be capable of shocking amounts of violence, and many, assuming their innocent nature, fall victim to them. In Coral Springs, Florida in 1997 one such story took place. And still the actions of the evening resonate throughout the community.

In The Beginning

Born in 1979 to a mother that didn't want her, Jacquiline "Nikki" Reynolds was adopted by Robert and Billie Jean Reynolds three months after her birth. The Reynolds were a loving, Christian family from Coral Springs, Florida and they were delighted to welcome their new daughter into their lives.

There was nothing that they wouldn't do for Nikki. Robert Reynolds worked for the Department of Transportation and Billie Jean was an administrative assistant at RJ Reynolds. They had a quiet home and they were devoted to making their daughter happy.

Nikki was a good child. She was devoted to the church, like her parents, and she loved her parents deeply. She would go to the mall with her mother or watch baseball games with her father. She could never spend too much time with them. The Reynolds did everything to ensure that Nikki was being raised in a loving and non-judgmental environment.

Friends and family would agree that the environment was loving, but the Reynolds gave Nikki everything she wanted. She was pampered, she was spoiled, and in the end, she was a bit of a brat. Sometimes the best intentions can have the worst consequences.

Still, Nikki, as she got older, became a good student and didn't act out. She achieved good grades in school and went out of her way to become involved in extra curricular activities. She also stayed heavily involved with the church alongside her parents.

By all appearances, Nikki was the perfect child. She was the child that most parents dream of having and Robert and Billie Jean were delighted with her. But children grow up, despite anything that their parents try to do to stop it, and Nikki was no exception. And not all children grow up in a manner that their parents can be proud of.

The Beginning of the End

Nikki went from being the model child to what most people would call a 'troubled teen'. It didn't start in the way one would expect, with failing grades and a lack of interest in school. It started with a lie, and one that shocked family and friends in the disturbing nature of it.

In 1996, sixteen-year-old Nikki came home from school and claimed that she had been assaulted after getting off of the school bus. Naturally her parents were shocked and appalled to hear that this had happened to her. They immediately called the police to handle the situation officially. Nikki claimed she had been attacked by someone she knew, at first. But when questioned by the police her story quickly changed.

She went on to say that she didn't know her attacker and then that the attack hadn't happened at all. She hadn't been raped. She'd made the whole story up.

Now why would a sixteen-year-old, devote Christian girl make up a story about being raped? Why would she go to the extreme of telling her parents and getting the police involved if it was just a story?

It turns out that Nikki hadn't been raped. Rather she was in a relationship, the first one of a sexual nature in her lifetime, and she was terrified to tell her parents about it. She was worried about what they would think about their daughter sacrificing her morals and her principles just to have a boyfriend. But Carlos Infante was her entire world. The sixteen-year-old classmate was consuming her life focus to the point that she hadn't hesitated to throw caution to the wind.

And when the thought of telling her parents about what was going on had come up, in her mind, fabricating a rape story had seemed like a better idea. Nikki was also concerned that she might be pregnant, a worry that was quickly put to rest, but it also influenced her decision to pursue the rape narrative.

Billie Jean was extremely unhappy with Nikki, potentially for the first time during her parenting of the girl. She didn't like the fact that Nikki had a boyfriend. She didn't like the fact that she'd sacrificed her principles and morals, the beliefs that they thought they'd instilled into her all for some boy. They believed that they'd raised a good, Christian girl and for the first time they were starting to question that belief.

Bille Jean and Robert disliked the idea of Nikki having a boyfriend, it didn't particularly matter who he was. They viewed it as a step down for her. They saw it as a complete abandonment of her belief system, something they had strived to instill in her over the course of her entire life. She was sacrificing everything in order to be with this boy, from their point of view. She was losing herself in him. And Billie Jean and Robert wanted to help get Nikki back on a clear path, on a Christian path.

So, they insisted that she spend less time with Carlos and more time with the church. They hoped that in doing so she would see her wrongdoings and find her true self again. They hoped that in spending more time with the church that she would become closer to the family again and forget about Carlos.

Billie Jean believed that Nikki needed to spend more time with a better group of people, a Christian group of people. She hoped that if Nikki spent time around other good, Christian kids that she would find her way again, that she would find a better crowd. And Billie Jean was willing to go to great lengths to ensure that her daughter found a path that fit with the beliefs and morals of the family.

But sometimes the child, no matter how much they push, cannot realize the hopes and dreams of parents. And sometimes, despite all efforts, things still go wrong.

Rebellion Continues

Teenage rebellion can be a strong force, however, and the more that Billie Jean pushed Nikki to go to church the more she resisted. Nikki said, "I knew that the way I was living was not right in God's eyes, but I did not want to hear all of that." She was too engulfed in her life with Carlos. He was quickly becoming her entire world and nothing else mattered to her. Not her parents, and certainly not her church.

The rebellion was extending into her school life. Nikki, who had once been a good student with marks that her parents could be proud of was now beginning to skip class. Her grades were beginning to fall as a result and she was no longer the academic force that she was before.

It was to the point that Billie Jean and Robert barely recognized the girl that they had raised anymore. Who was this young woman living in their house? She reflected none of the morals and principles they had raised her to uphold. She wouldn't listen to them. She opposed them at every turn. They began to wonder what had happened to their daughter Nikki. Where had she gone?

Nikki went from a happy-go-lucky child that was a pleasure to be around, a child who was soft spoken and loved to go to church to a girl no one could recognize. She wore dark clothes, she changed her music, she changed her bedroom to dark colours – she became the opposite of herself. It was hard to tell if this was simply teenage rebellion or something more going on. Was this all because of Carlos or was there some deeper problem at play?

She slept a lot, more than any teenager should and she isolated herself from her family. Gone were the days of ice cream and base ball games. She no longer went on trips to the mall with her mother. She no longer went to church with her family. She became disinterested in many things that used to hold her attention, things that used to captivate her. Her whole world now revolved around Carlos.

It was her first sexual relationship with anyone in her life and it had reached the point of obsession. She filled her diary with everything to do with Carlos. Her room was plastered with photos of him. Her every waking moment revolved around him. There was an unnatural intensity to her emotions towards him, an unhealthy intensity. And it was quickly becoming evident that this was a problem.

Naturally, Billie Jean and Robert were very concerned about their daughter's current mental state. She was not herself, and the only thing they could blame was Carlos as he was the only changing factor in her life. It seemed that he was a negative influence on Nikki in many ways. He didn't make good grades as a student, and now her grades were plummeting as well.

Billie Jean was also worried that he was coming over every day, potentially when they were at work. They had no way to confirm this, but she didn't like the idea that he was at the house alone with her while they were at work. It didn't sit well with her.

So Billie Jean put her foot down, perhaps for the first time in her experience as a parent. She began to tell Nikki no, especially when it came to Carlos. And Nikki handled it with the maturity level of a toddler as opposed to that of a teenager. Nikki threw awful tantrums. Billie Jean and Nikki would engage in screaming matches in the house that would result in slammed doors. The result was very wearing on Billie Jean. She found herself screaming at Nikki almost all of the time. This was not what she wanted her life as a mother to be. This was not the girl she had raised. She needed to do something about this, but she was at a loss as to what the solution could be.

And despite the screaming matches and the orders to stay away, Nikki still kept seeing Carlos. It seemed that nothing could keep her from Carlos. She would sneak out at night when everyone was asleep to see him and it didn't matter what the consequences were.

Billie Jean's frustration escalated to the point that one day she confided in a friend saying "Don't be surprised if one day you come home and there's police cars and fire trucks up and down the street 'cause one of us, it'll be me or Nikki, but one of us will be gone."

Billie Jean's prediction would prove to hit a little too close to home in the coming days. And the aftermath would shock everyone.

Intervention

It was May 14, 1997 when the school counselor contacted Billie Jean to tell her that there was trouble with Nikki and Carlos. She asked that Billie Jean come in and speak with her in person and that Billie Jean, Robert, and Nikki come in for a full meeting the next day. Upon visiting the high school, the counselor told Billie Jean that Nikki and Carlos had more than just the usual high school relationship issues to deal with.

That day Nikki had told the counselor that she was pregnant with Carlos' baby. This had naturally prompted the counselor to contact Billie Jean immediately about the issue. Billie Jean, having already dealt with Nikki's questionable honesty with the previous rape accusation, was hesitant to believe the pregnancy claim. She was fairly certain that this was another one of Nikki's schemes, but there was a sure way to determine its legitimacy.

So she took Nikki to the drug store to find out what was what.

The results of the pregnancy test were negative. That didn't mean Billie Jean was any less pleased with her daughter. Nikki called Carlos with the news. And despite having a counseling meeting the next day Billie Jean decided to seek guidance from a higher power. She dragged Nikki away from the phone and took Nikki to see the church counselor.

Nikki spoke with her pastor as they waited to see the counselor. He was supportive as he talked to her about her boyfriend problems and offered her guidance. Their conversation with the counselor did not have the same supportive tone. The counselor spent the session telling Nikki that her mother did not deserve the behaviour she was displaying. She raised her voice and yelled at Nikki. This didn't go over very well.

Nikki removed herself from the office and from the church. She wanted nothing more to do with the impromptu counseling session. And as she stood in the parking lot of the church she even debated removing herself from the family by running away. But she didn't run away, however. Instead, she took a higher ground, something that hadn't been seen from her in almost a year. She went back into the counselor's office and apologized to her mother. And she finished the session with the counselor before returning home with her mother.

Billie Jean believed that they had made a step in the right direction. She would be the one to learn how wrong she was about that fact.

Confusion and Confessions

It was barely an hour after their visit to the counselor on May 14, 1997 that the call came in to 911. At 7:07pm Nikki Reynolds' panicked voice came over the phone saying "I stabbed her repeatedly in the back. There's blood all over her and all over the floor and everything."

Police were at her house in minutes and the scene that they witnessed was one that would stay with some of the officers for years after. When police arrived they found Nikki waiting on her doorstep. One of the officers who responded indicated that "She had blood all over, blood on her legs, blood on her face."

Nikki was placed in the back of the police car and left to wait while the police went to investigate. A tape recorder was left on with her in the police car so that anything that was said while she was alone was recorded and on file. It recorded her praying that her mother was still be alive and saying that she had learned her lesson. She was asking God to forgive her and for her mother to please still be alive.

Her mother was brought out of the house on a stretcher by the EMTs and she was still alive at the time that she left the house. However, Billie Jean was pronounced dead at the hospital at 8:10pm after suffering from 13 stab wounds.

Nikki was taken to the police department immediately. Robert came home from work to find the house in a state of chaos, surrounded by police cars and police tape. He hadn't yet been informed of the situation that had come to pass behind the front doors of his home. He broke down at the news that his wife was gone and that his daughter was responsible. The shock of it was something that he couldn't quite comprehend.

The scene inside the house was gruesome and shocking to police investigators. It depicted Billie Jean's terrible, drawn out death as she fought to get away from her daughter. But there was no escape for her as she was stabbed repeatedly until she finally lay immobile on the floor.

The police found the kitchen knife that had been used as the murder weapon in the sink and it still had blood on it. They also found evidence that someone, likely Nikki, had attempted to clean up the scene using towels and dishcloths. The blood soaked pieces of cloth were scattered about the kitchen unable to handle the sheer amount of blood that had resulted from the incident.

While the police officers worked diligently at the crime seen the detectives questioned Nikki about the murder. And it didn't take too much effort to get her to talk.

"I didn't have any intentions of lying." Nikki said. "I didn't have any secrets. I wanted to get it out." She felt almost compelled to tell the story of what had happened. She needed to let them know.

"It was simple, all I had to ask her was what happened today and just started chatting. She went through the whole story from a to b," said the detective who interviewed Nikki.

The story that was told by Nikki revolved heavily around Carlos Infante, the infamous boyfriend. Nikki had used her fake pregnancy to keep Carlos in a relationship with her when he wanted to leave, fearing what would happen if he left. When she had found out she was not pregnant, for sure, she called him to give the news. Carlos indicated that he wanted nothing to do with her and all of her lies. He'd had enough. Billie Jean had even got on the phone with Carlos and apologized for all of the drama that he'd had to endure at the hands of her daughter.

Nikki had decided then and there that someone would die that day. She even took a handful of aspirin before going to the counseling meeting with her mother at the church. She was certain that she could overdose on it. She was certain that it would be her that would die.

However, when the overdose failed her thoughts went from suicide to homicide rather quickly. But the intended victim had not been her mother.

Her plan had been to get a hold of Carlos the next day and kill him. She figured she could catch him after first hour and slash his throat if she snuck up behind him. She believed that if she couldn't have him then no one should be allowed to have him. He belonged to her essentially.

However, the one obstacle in her plan to kill Carlos was the meeting they had with the guidance counselor the next day. Nikki was unsure whether she would be sent home after the meeting or not. In order to kill Carlos she would have to skip the guidance meeting. So, in order to accomplish this, she figured she would have to kill her parents as well. She would just wait until they were sleeping and then simply slash their throats. Then they could no longer stand in her way.

A real obstacle came into this metaphorical plan when her father left for church after dinner that night alone and her mother stayed home. This was very out of character for them. Nikki also stayed home as her mother told her she was grounded for the rest of the evening. She was instructed to clean the dishes after dinner.

Nikki decided that she would just roll with this change. She believed, since she was now home alone with her mother, that it would be much easier to kill her mother now, clean up the mess, and then wait until her father returned. She could then kill him and do the same. Finally, she could drive herself to school in the morning, wait for Carlos, and kill him after first hour just like she had planned. It would work out perfectly.

Logical thought was gone at this point in time. Nikki was acting strictly on whatever thoughts came to her mind and they were frantic, desperate. Still, she waited for her opportunity to arrive. She waited for her moment when she could kill her mother.

Opportunity came while she was cleaning up in the kitchen and Billie Jean was working at her computer. Nikki took a kitchen knife, paused for a moment to check the blade for its sharpness, and then slowly approached her mother. She hesitated now that she had the knife in hand. She wasn't sure what it would feel like to slash someone's throat.

When she finally got up the nerve to come up behind her mother and attempt to cut her throat it didn't slash it, it only cut it. Billie Jean jumped up in surprise and darted towards the laundry room. She screamed, "No, Nikki, no."

"I told her I had to kill her because I can't live without Carlos," Nikki explained to police in her interview.

Nikki kept stabbing her because she wanted to put her out of her misery, she claims. She didn't want her mother to suffering any longer. And in her last moments, Billie Jean still offered her daughter forgiveness for killing her.

Nikki spent one night in the hospital because of her claim of ingesting a large amount of Aspirin. After that she was turned over to the county jail where she was formally booked on a charge of First Degree Murder.

The First Trial

The first trial for Nikki Reynolds lasted from April 14, 1999 – May 3, 1999.

If convicted, Nikki faced life in prison after spending two years in a Juvenile Detention Centre. The prosecution built their case around Nikki's obsession with Carlos Infante, making sure to indicate that he was not at fault in any way and rather he was also one of the three listed on Nikki's kill list.

The defence opted to take an insanity plea route, rather than try to dispute the charge that Nikki had committed the murder – something she had confessed to multiple times. This defence fell flat. The criterion for an insanity plea is very strict. The accused has to suffer from a serious mental illness and the accused has to be unaware that what they are doing is wrong or has consequences.

The psychologist that testified for the prosecution indicated that Nikki was well aware of what she was doing, and rather that she was just a confused girl. The defence tried to argue that Nikki suffered from Borderline Personality disorder. They claimed that individuals suffering from this disorder could idolize the individuals they are with and then suddenly snap, and become violent. Which is very similar to Nikki's reaction after Carlos indicated he wanted nothing to do with her. They also claimed that the Aspirin played a part as Aspirin can cause metabolic imbalances and psychosis upon overdoes.

Regardless of the claims on either side, the jury was hung and the trial ended in a mistrial.

The Second Trial

Second trail for Nikki Reynolds began on Sept 1, 1999.

Similar to the first, the prosecution brought a series of psychologists to the stand to prove that, while not a rational act, Nikki was not insane. The prosecution also claimed that her mother's death was premeditated.

The defence countered that Nikki was mentally ill and called experts to speak to Nikki's sanity. The defence also brought forward Nikki's biological mother to testify. The birth mother had a long history of mental illness and family violence. The defence argued that it was the anxiety over losing Carlos that pushed Nikki over the edge and brought her mental illness to the surface.

After much deliberation, Nikki Reynolds was found guilty of Second Degree Murder at the end of the trial.

At the sentencing hearing on January 7, 2000 Nikki's biological mother made a plea to include treatment as a part of Nikki's sentence. She believed that her daughter needed help, much like she had needed help in her lifetime.

Nikki also addressed the court, pleading with the judge to sentence her to a psychiatric facility instead of prison. She truly believed that there had been something wrong that day, if not insanity, than something else. She believed that she needed help. She bore no ill will towards her family. She hated none of them. She had never hated them and still didn't.

However, the judge believed that the wrongness of what she had done to outweigh all else. He gave her the maximum sentence under Florida law, 34 years in prison. She was resentenced to 21 years and 8 months on April 4, 2001 due to a change in sentencing laws in the state of Florida.

In the end Robert Reynolds remarried in 1998 and has had no contact with his daughter since she was sent to prison on January 2000.

And Nikki was incarcerated at the Gadsden Correctional Facility in Quincy, Florida. She was eligible for parole in 2015 and was released.